A SHORT HISTORY OF THE ROYAL MARINES

1664 – 2004

Published by
The Royal Marines Historical Society

Special Publication No 29

First Edition 2002
Reprinted 2003
Second Revised Edition 2004

Printed by Holbrooks Printers, Norway Road, Portsmouth, Hants. PO3 5HX

© RMHS 2004

ISBN 0 9536163 3 9

1

Introduction

This second, updated edition has been produced by the Royal Marines Historical Society as a compact historical guide to the Royal Marines for easy reference. It includes extensive appendices covering many aspects of Corps history.

The majority of the photographs are the copyright of the Royal Marines Museum. Our thanks to the late Charles Stadden, a member of the Society, for his approval to use paintings which were originally commissioned by the Royal Marines Museum. Thanks also go to Captain Derek Oakley MBE, Major Alastair Donald and Major Mark Bentinck for the text; also to members of the serving Corps for help with more recent history up to and including the 21st century campaigns in Afghanistan and Iraq.

There are large numbers of published books relating to the history of the Royal Marines since 1664, most of which are available for deeper research in the Corps Museum archives at Eastney, Portsmouth. A selected bibliography is at Appendix X.

The Royal Marines Historical Society would like to acknowledge the following authors whose works were used extensively in this booklet: Gen Sir H E Blumberg, Richard Brooks, Col C Field, Col G Grover, A Cecil Hampshire, James D Ladd, Maj Gen J M Moulton, Capt D A Oakley, Col Markham Rose, Peter C Smith and Maj Gen J H A Thompson.

The Royal Marines Historical Society was formed in 1964 and carries out research into all aspects of Corps history, working closely with the RM Museum. It publishes newsletters, journals and special booklets. (see page 160)

Meticulous readers will find some inconsistency between the use of 'Marines' and 'marines', but the continual use of 'Royal Marines' is too cumbersome. There is also some inconsistency in the abbreviation of ranks. The authors have taken liberties as they deem appropriate.

Contents

Chapter 1   The Early Marine Regiments – 1664-1755 7
Chapter 2   Three Grand Divisions – 1755-1827 12
Chapter 3   Crimea, Boers & Boxers – 1827-1902 20
Chapter 4   Early Twentieth Century – 1902-1939 30
Chapter 5   Second World War – 1939-1945 52
Chapter 6   Reorganisation & Deployments – 1945-1951 63
Chapter 7   More Brush Fire Wars – 1952-1970 68
Chapter 8   The End of the Empire – 1970-1981 76
Chapter 9   The Falklands War – 1982 86
Chapter 10   The Gulf War and a New Century – 1983-2002 95
Chapter 11   International Terrorism – Afghanistan and Iraq........... 105

Appendix A   The Colours 120
Appendix B   Memorable Dates 124
Appendix C   Senior Royal Marines Appointments 128
Appendix D   Royal Marines Organisation 2004 129
Appendix E   The Victoria Cross 130
Appendix F   Honours and Awards 132
Appendix G   The Wilkinson Sword of Peace 133
Appendix H   The King's Squad 134
Appendix I   Freedoms and Privileges 135
Appendix J   Royal Marines Prayers 136
Appendix K   Associations with City Livery Companies 137
Appendix L   Associations with Other Marine Corps 138
Appendix M   Associations with Other Regiments 140
Appendix N   Regimental Music 142
Appendix O   Nicknames and Sayings 144
Appendix P   Royal Marines Museum 145
Appendix Q   Mess Customs 146
Appendix R   Specialist Qualification Badges 147
Appendix S   Lanyards 148
Appendix T   The Green Beret 148
Appendix U   The Royal Marines Association 149
Appendix V   The Royal Marines Reserve 150
Appendix W   Cadets 150
Appendix X   Bibliography 152
Appendix Y   A Brief Chronology of Principal Events 154
Appendix Z   *"Soldier an' Sailor Too"* 159

Royal Marines Historical Society Publications............. 160

Genealogical Tree of The Royal Marines

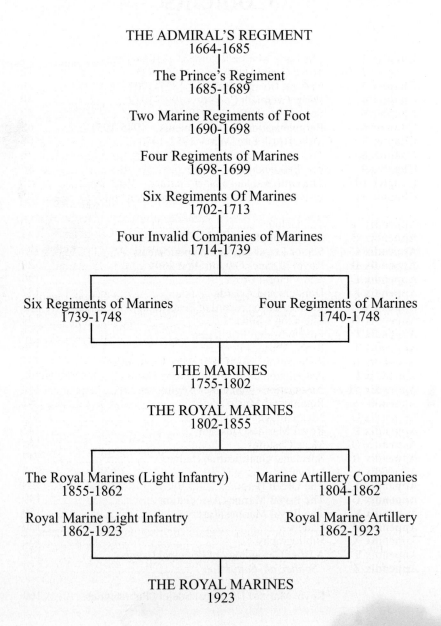

THE ADMIRAL'S REGIMENT
1664-1685

The Prince's Regiment
1685-1689

Two Marine Regiments of Foot
1690-1698

Four Regiments of Marines
1698-1699

Six Regiments Of Marines
1702-1713

Four Invalid Companies of Marines
1714-1739

Six Regiments of Marines   Four Regiments of Marines
1739-1748   1740-1748

THE MARINES
1755-1802

THE ROYAL MARINES
1802-1855

The Royal Marines (Light Infantry)   Marine Artillery Companies
1855-1862   1804-1862

Royal Marine Light Infantry   Royal Marine Artillery
1862-1923   1862-1923

THE ROYAL MARINES
1923

Foreword to the Second Revised Edition

by Major General Julian Thompson CB, OBE

"We have compelled every land and every sea to open up a path for our valour, and have everywhere planted eternal memorials of our friendship and our enmity."

Pericles

The Author of a recent history of the Royal Marines compared them with the French Foreign Legion, remarking that both gained their reputations after years of gruelling service in far corners of the world, often unheard, unseen, and too frequently unappreciated. Both the Royal Marines and the Foreign Legion are famous for their ability to turn their hands to anything. The unofficial motto of the Legion, which might be translated; 'get yourself out of trouble because no else is going to', could equally have applied to the Royal Marines many times in what Winston Churchill called their 'long, rough, glorious history'.

The first edition of the Short History of the Royal Marines, published in 2002, was long overdue; especially for recruits and young officers for whom time is at a premium. The fact-filled book by Derek Oakley, Alastair Donald and Mark Bentinck filled the bill admirably. That the Royal Marines Historical Society has felt the need to bring out this revised version a mere two years after publishing the first edition is eloquent testimony to how busy the Corps has been and continues to be. To have fitted 340 busy years of Royal Marines operations and activity into 160 pages is no mean feat. This edition contains even more information than its predecessor on the traditions and many other aspects of Corps life. It will continue to provide answers to the most searching questions, not only aimed by instructors at young men under training, but also to the general public and to any serving or retired Royal Marines, however senior.

We live in an age in which many, especially in the media and other opinion-forming bodies, denigrate the past as mere sentiment at best and an unwelcome bar to progress at worst. While it is true that past performance is no guarantee of future execution and mere imitation of one's predecessor's actions and methods may be unproductive, standards and ethos can be a guide when in danger or in doubt.

Generations of our predecessors have 'been there' before; whether on the bullet-swept decks of ships under sail, in the turrets and transmitting stations of warships in both World Wars, wading ashore in numerous landings with the cold sea behind and potential disaster staring them in the face, in helicopters, landing craft and amphibians of many kinds. In the end so often in what a United States Marine called 'LPCs' or 'leather personnel carriers', boots, they have 'yomped' to close with the enemy in every kind of terrain imaginable from the beaches of Normandy to the landing zones of the El Faw Peninsula and the road to Basra. The Royal Marines of today are but the most recent inheritors of a tradition in which to give one's all to achieve the objective is ingrained and to whom failure is not an option. On occasions, disaster, chaos, yes; our past does not lack examples of these, but stories of how Royal Marines have risen above these abound, and many are covered in this book. I commend it to all serving and ex-Royal Marines as well as to the general public who may find the story of what Winston Churchill called 'the greatest Corps in the World' of interest.

The RM Memorial in the Mall, London, rededicated in 2000 as the RM National Memorial to commemorate also over 600 Royal Marines killed on active service all around the Globe since World War 2.

6

Chapter 1

The Early Marine Regiments
1664-1755

The Royal Marines are the soldiers of the Royal Navy and can trace their descent from a regiment specially raised and trained for service with the Navy and paid by the Admiralty.

It was the outbreak of the Second Dutch War in 1664 that a regiment of 1,200 men, commanded by Colonel Sir William Killigrew, was ordered to be formed in the City of London. The men were recruited for service to the 'Navy Royall and Admiralty' and the regiment was named after the Lord High Admiral himself, Charles II's brother, James, who was fitting out a fleet to face the Dutch in Home waters. Defined as 'Land Souldjers' the regiment was known as the Duke of York and Albany's Maritime Regiment of Foot and the Order in Council was dated 28th October 1664.

James was a strict disciplinarian and welcomed a regiment that would help with his manning problem and bring personal loyalty to the fleet. It had been the practice for 200 years for ships of the Royal Navy to be paid off in peace and crews impressed from the seafaring population in times of emergency. When war was declared in February 1665, the English Fleet sailed under James and met the Dutch off Lowestoft in a fierce battle that left both fleets incapable of further action. This was the first action by the new regiment who were strikingly arrayed in uniforms of yellow coats with red facings, sashes and stockings and were all armed with flintlock muskets, instead of some with pikes as in other regiments. Yellow was the favourite colour of the Duke.

It was often known as The Admiral's Regiment, until James was forced to resign as Lord High Admiral in 1673, when his Regiment became referred to as The Duke's Regiment. The Colonel was licensed by the Lord Mayor of London to recruit from within the City and many were from the Trained Bands, the City's own volunteer militia. It is from this origin that the Royal Marines today derive the privilege, enjoyed by very few regiments, of marching through the

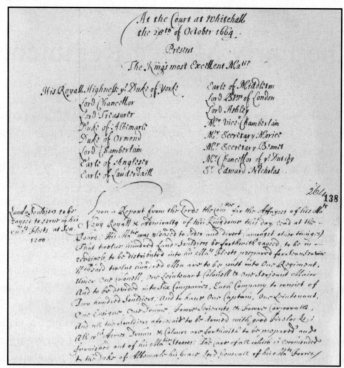

Privy Council Proceedings authorising 1200 soldiers to be raised for sea service

City with Colours flying, drums beating and bayonets fixed. The first use of the term 'Marines' that has been traced is in a letter written by Captain Sylas Taylor of the regiment in 1672 after the Battle of Solebay.

When Charles II died in 1685, his brother came to the throne as James II and the Regiment passed to Prince George, James's son-in-law and the husband of his second daughter, Anne. The Regiment was titled Prince George of Denmark's Maritime Regiment, but better known as The Prince's Regiment. However James's reign as a Catholic king was short lived and William of Orange, was invited to England in the Protestant cause. Many army regiments went over to William, but the Prince's Regiment, commanded by an ardent royalist for over 20 years, remained loyal to James. After he fled to France in 1689, William with his wife Mary, James's eldest daughter, were declared joint sovereigns. The Regiment was considered to be

8

too favourable to the previous regime and consequently disbanded, its men being incorporated into the Coldstream Guards.

Almost immediately Britain was again at war with France, and the following year two Marine Regiments were raised by the Earls of Torrington and Pembroke as the 1st and 2nd Regiments of Marines. Although the men of these Regiments served in the Fleet in all the sea battles of the war, ashore in Jamaica, at the siege of Cork in Ireland and in France, after the Peace of Ryswick both regiments were disbanded in 1699.

The War of the Spanish Succession broke out in 1702 and a number of regiments were raised, six of them as Marines and each known by the name of their Colonel, Saunderson's, Villiers's, Fox's, Mordaunt's, Holt's and Shannon's. These regiments fought in Spain, France and North America and most of them were involved, with 400 Dutch Marines, in the Capture and Defence of Gibraltar in 1704, of which a contemporary author wrote "The garrison did more than could be humanly expected and the British Marines gained immortal honour". At the Treaty of Utrecht in 1713, the last three regiments were disbanded, whilst the first three were reformed as line infantry, later becoming the East Lancashire Regiment, the East Surrey Regiment and the Duke of Cornwall's Light Infantry, and all of which are justly proud of their origins as Marines.

Once again there were no Regiments of Marines. From the time of the accession of George I in 1714, it was only four companies of marine invalids which kept the name alive. Formed for garrison duties, the companies were found from men of the former Marine Regiments, who were no longer fit for active service.

It was not until 1739, when war with Spain broke out again, known as the War of Jenkin's Ear, that marines properly reappeared on the scene. When George II addressed Parliament and announced that "In the prosecution of this war a number of soldiers to serve on board the fleet may be requisite, and I have judged it proper that a body of Marines should be raised", it was greeted with loud applause. Six Regiments of Marines were formed and were joined by another four the following year. During almost the whole of the next decade Marines experienced highs and lows, fighting in the Caribbean, including the disastrous attack on Cartagena, they sailed round the

The capture of Gibraltar by British and Dutch Marines in 1704

world with Anson, during the '45 Rebellion they were at Culloden, and in India they took part in the Siege of Pondicherry, where the well-documented female marine, Hannah Snell, was severely wounded *(see her memoirs right)*.

Service in the Marines had become unpopular; by 1745 when a first commission cost only £250-£280 compared to the £500 for officers of the Line. The Admiralty budget for 1747-48 provided for 40,000 seamen and 11,550 marines. Although the Peace of Aix-la-Chapelle, signed in 1748, was merely a temporary truce in the long conflict with France, the Marine Regiments were nevertheless again disbanded.

This was the last time they were disbanded, for what had become known as the War of the Austrian Succession had finally emphasised a requirement that had built up over the eighty or so years during most of which Marines had existed. It had shown the necessity for a permanent body of troops specially raised and equipped for sea service. This force was required in order to provide landing parties from ships to destroy enemy fleets inshore, to engage in combined operations and to provide protection ashore whenever the fleet needed to take on provisions or water in unfriendly territory. It was

Hannah Snell published her memoirs of service

also realised that there was an administrative factor to be addressed. At this time sailors were not usually paid until the end of the commission whereas soldiers were normally clothed and regularly paid by the Colonel of their Regiment. However when an army regiment was split up among ships of the Fleet, this was seldom possible. Consequently it was necessary to have a force organised with sufficiently elastic administration to compete with these requirements. Admiral Lord Anson pressed for the formation of a permanent body of Marines under Admiralty control and organised on a company basis.

The historian G M Trevelyan wrote:

"It is remarkable how soon they (the Marines) acquired two reputations that clung to them for many generations – a reputation for good, honest service and character, and a reputation among snobs of being socially less smart than the army"

Chapter 2

Three Grand Divisions
1755-1827

In 1755, as war clouds again began to threaten, Parliament voted an establishment of 5,000 Marines and with Lord Anson as First Lord of the Admiralty, an Order-in-Council provided for fifty independent companies organised into three Divisions at the naval ports of Chatham, Portsmouth and Plymouth. This new organisation set the pattern for the future of the Corps and lasted up until after the Second World War. Many of the experienced officers and some of the NCOs for the first of these companies had served in the regiments disbanded in 1748. Officers were now commissioned into a definite company, recruiting parties were sent out from the Divisions and in due course detachments were sent off to sea with, it must be said, very little training at that time. These detachments varied in size from a hundred in a first-rate ship of the line, down to twenty in a small frigate.

The Seven Years War with France broke out the following year, but when Byng was sent with a Fleet to relieve Minorca and for the raids that were being made on the French coast, there were not enough Marines to go round and army regiments had to be embarked. However, by 1758 the strength of the Marines had been increased to 14,845 in 100 companies and Marines then served in Boscawen's fleet off Lagos, with Hawke at Quiberon Bay and in an amphibious operation they captured Senegal. Later that year, led by James Wolfe, who had been first commissioned in one of the previous Marine Regiments in 1741, they fought at Cape Breton and St John's, thus giving the French good reason to doubt their own future in Canada. Eventually at Quebec a battalion of Marines, which included Robert Ross, who was later to play a leading role in Australia, created a diversion and allowed Wolfe's force to scale the Heights of Abraham and capture the city, thereby securing Canada for Britain.

The increased strength of the Marines allowed two battalions of Marines, one from barracks and one from the Fleet to be formed during Keppel's expedition to Belle Isle in 1761. They played a decisive part in the capture of this island off the coast of France on 7th June. On 22nd April, after an earlier landing had failed. Grenadiers of the 19th Regiment and a company of Marines scaled the cliffs at La Maria in a diversionary attack. Although fiercely attacked by the French, they held their positions until relieved by the remainder of the battalion. This then became the main landing and the French defences were overrun. Asked afterwards what troops has been most effective against them the French replied 'les petits grenadiers', meaning the Marines who wore grenadier caps but who were not as tall as the men in army grenadier companies. It was subsequently written *"The Marines gained immortal glory............"* and it is believed that the laurel wreath, which forms part of the insignia of the Corps, was awarded to honour the part played by the Marines in the capture of Belle Isle, and which today is one of the memorable dates celebrated by the Corps *(see Appendix B)*.

By the time Spain entered the war in 1762, the voted strength had gradually risen to over 19,000, and it was the new and far more flexible organisation that enabled the Admiralty to manage the administration of this expansion by gradually increasing the number of companies at each of the three Divisions, and which by then had reached an overall total of 135. This ultimately must have provided sufficient detachments at sea, because it was possible to form two further battalions which were engaged in the capture of Havana.

Around the Globe with Napoleon – 1770-1815

The Seven Years War had left France waiting to avenge her defeat and the American colonists, relieved of the French threat from Canada, were able to express their resentment of home authority by resorting to violence. In 1773 the famous Boston Tea Party was the climax of the American colonists resistance to British taxation and led them to sever the ties with the mother country two years later with the American Revolution.

A Marine battalion under Major Pitcairn was sent to Boston and on 19th April 1775 the opening shots of the American War of Independence were fired by a detachment of his Marines at

13

Bunker Hill taken by the Marines and the 47th Regiment in 1775

Lexington. Further Marines arrived in May and were formed into another battalion. After seeing action at Lexington and Concord, some 750 Marines reached Boston on 20th May. Here they were formed into two battalions, the 1st Marines under Major Short and the 2nd Marines commanded by Major Tupper, with Major John Pitcairn in overall command. On 17th June they were engaged in driving the rebels from their positions on the top of Bunker Hill at the point of the bayonet. In the closing stages of the battle, in the face of a deadly volley their commander was mortally wounded. It is said that imitation is the sincerest form of flattery and therefore it must be recorded that on 10th November 1775 the Continental Congress formed a Marine Corps, a force with which today the Corps has a strong affiliation *(see Appendix L)*.

On the other side of the world, a small Marine detachment was with Captain Cook when he landed at Botany Bay in 1770, but it was in 1788 that Marines started to play a major part in the founding of Australia. A large contingent of 21 officers and 192 men commanded by Major Robert Ross, along with 45 wives and children accompanied the first convicts and were present when the Union flag was raised with due ceremony at Sydney Cove. Ross became the first

14

Marines were with Captain Cook when he claimed a British Possession at Botany Bay, 1770

Lieutenant Governor of New South Wales and then of Norfolk Island. After disagreement with Governor Arthur Phillip about the poor pay and conditions of Marines he returned to England in 1791. Captain David Collins, another veteran of Bunker Hill, was appointed the Judge Advocate subsequently becoming Lieutenant Governor in Tasmania in 1803. As colonisation of Australia continued, many Marines took their discharge and formed the nucleus of the first settlers.

When France declared war on Britain in 1793 following the Revolution the Navy found itself extremely short not only of seamen, but also of Marines. In consequence a number of infantry regiments again served at sea in ships of the line, whilst Marines were mainly sent to frigates and sloops. These are the army regiments, which today are proud of the honours and traditions they observe in their historic dates, badges, and in some cases even music, and which are derived from the time they spent at sea. Detachments of these regiments, together with those of the Marines, fought in the Battles of the Glorious First of June, Cape St Vincent and Camperdown, and shared in Nelson's victories at the Nile and Copenhagen. Indeed on 1st June 1794 when Lord Howe met and decisively defeated a similar sized French fleet, thirteen of his ships carried Marine detachments.

By 1801, out of a Navy Vote of 135,000 men, nearly 23,000 were Marines, later to be increased to over 30,000.When the war was over in 1802 the Corps reduced to 12,119.

That year was a memorable one as it was probably not only the meritorious service of the Marines that resulted in the Corps being granted the title 'Royal', but also their loyalty at the time of the great naval mutinies of Spithead and the Nore in 1797. On 29th April Lord St Vincent, First Lord of the Admiralty, announced that His Majesty King George III had been pleased to direct that in future the Corps should now be styled the 'Royal Marines'. Orders were given that their new uniforms, scarlet with blue facings, were to be delivered in time for the anniversary of the King's Birthday on 4th June. At Plymouth when they assumed these new uniforms, a large crowd cheered when they saw them parade, the barracks were illuminated and a grand ball held in their honour. Later Lord St Vincent said:

"In obtaining for them the distinction of 'Royal' I but inefficiently did my duty. I never knew an appeal made to them for honour, courage or loyalty, that they did not more than realize my highest expectations. If ever the hour of real danger should come to England, they will be found the country's sheet anchor."

From the middle of the eighteenth century Royal Artillery detachments had been embarked to man the large mortars in bomb vessels. However, because they did not consider themselves subject to the Naval Discipline Act and would not undertake ship's duties, there was friction between them and the Naval Officers on board. By 1804 the crisis had come to a head and, largely at the instigation of Lord Nelson, an artillery company was formed at each of the Royal Marine Divisions on 18th August. When a fourth Division was established at Woolwich the following year, an artillery company was formed there also. It was not until 1862 that the Royal Marine Artillery was formed into a separate Division, and work was started on a purpose-built barracks for it at Eastney, Southsea, Hampshire and its officers were separately listed.

Trafalgar and War with America

War had broken out again with France in May 1803 and Napoleon began to amass the *Grande Armee*. Once again the Navy

Vote rose to 38,000 seamen and 12,000 marines and this had trebled by 1812.

On 21st October 1805 Nelson defeated the combined French and Spanish fleets off Cape Trafalgar. Over one eighth of the Corps were serving in Nelson's fleet, 90 officers and over 3,500 men. Captain Adair aboard HMS *Victory* was shot whilst repelling boarders. Another officer, 2nd Lt Roteley, described the scene as being *"like a hailstorm of bullets passing over our heads on the poop, where we had forty marines with small arms."* Marines fought in the rigging and on the guns. In the Fleet four officers and 113 men were killed with 14 officers and over 200 men wounded. After Nelson was hit, Sergeant Secker and other marines carried him below. When the French Admiral Villeneuve wished to surrender aboard the *Bucentaure* it was to an officer of the Royal Marines, Captain James Atcherley, that he first offered his sword. Thinking this was improper Atcherley declined in favour of his captain.

When Nelson was killed at Trafalgar he was carried below by Sergeant Secker

Thus Napoleon's dream of invasion had ended. But it was ten long years before peace was restored following Wellington's victory at Waterloo. Before then Marines had been involved in a large number of smaller actions both ashore and afloat. British expeditions occupied Sicily and attacked distant French, Spanish and Dutch colonies, from Cape Town to Copenhagen, from Barcelona to the Dardanelles. A Marine battalion landed on the island of Walcheren, another took Anholt in the Baltic and held it, Captain 'Fighting' Nicholls becoming the Governor. There were numerous landings, often up steep cliffs against highly motivated defenders, while acting as a covering force for the Army as at Corunna and Mondego.

Finally it was when Napoleon, on boarding *Bellerophon* to be transported to the island of St Helena, inspected the RM guard that he remarked *"One might do much with 100,000 soldiers such as these"*. Three RM battalions, each with an RMA company, were engaged in the War of 1812 with the United States of America. This war opened with a series of bloody frigate actions in which the British, having neglected gunnery since Trafalgar, were soundly beaten by the larger American frigates. It was in the first of these that a British Marine shot and killed Lt Bush of the United States Marine Corps and later, when the Shannon captured the USS *Chesapeake* off Boston *"Marine fought Marine on the decks of the Chesapeake"*. In June 1813 the 1st & 2nd Battalions, each with an artillery company, arrived from Spain. After the attack on Hampton they served in Canada where the Americans were threatening Montreal. They then saw action on Lakes Champlain and Ontario where they manned some of the gunboats. They also raided the shores of Chesapeake Bay and were with the force that defeated the Americans at Bladensburg. The Brigade Commander at Hampton, Lt Col Charles Napier (later General Sir Charles Napier in India), recorded:

"Never in my life have I seen soldiers like the Marine Artillery. We suffered much fatigue and hardship, but never was seen anything not admirable in these glorious soldiers. Should my life extend to antediluvian years their conduct at Little Hampton will not be forgotten by me. All honour to the memory of these brave men".

They were present when Washington was burnt in reprisal for the American sacking of Toronto. Baltimore was then besieged and from their base on Cumberland Island they carried out raids to divert

the American troops from the defence of Orleans. Meanwhile Major 'Fighting' Nicholls had landed in eastern Louisiana and raised Creek and Choctaw Indians against the Americans. Shortly afterwards peace was proclaimed and the Marines returned to England arriving a few weeks after Waterloo. It had been a long and varied campaign against the Americans in which Marines had been deployed in both land and sea actions.

When the Duke of Clarence (later King William IV) in 1827 presented Colours to each of the four Divisions their new design was similar to those of the Colours

HRH The Duke of Clarence. *From a painting by Sir Thomas Lawrence and A Morton*

carried today and much of the insignia borne was granted by King George IV at this time *(see Appendix A)*.

Chapter 3

Crimea, Boers & Boxers
1827-1902

In other minor wars that followed detachments from the Mediterranean Fleet saw action when Algiers was bombarded and burnt down in the war against piracy in 1816 and also when Marines were landed from the fleet in the battle of Navarino Bay in 1827. When Queen Victoria came to the throne a Royal Marine battalion and an artillery company were in action in Spain during the Carlist War. Soon afterwards Marines from the fleet were again landed and, reinforced from Britain to make two battalions, they fought alongside the Turks during the Turko-Egyptian War, 1839-41, to recapture Syria.

A battalion from the fleet served in the First China War in the 1840s when British shipping was threatened by fleets of Chinese war junks. The Imperial Government in Peking had banned the East India Company's opium trade and other British traders came under threat. Smuggling was tolerated on both sides, but erupted with expulsions and attacks on shipping in the Pearl River. On 23rd May 1841 Captain Ellis led 380 Marines in the capture of the Bogue Forts guarding the approach to Canton and occupied Hong Kong, after which a truce was declared, an indemnity paid and the Marines re-embarked. In all about 700 Marines fought in the war with minor actions at Chusan, Amoy and Shanghai. The final engagement of the war involved some 200 Marines in a blistering attack on the walled city of Chinkiang Foo.

RM detachments fought ashore in the Maori Wars in New Zealand in 1845 and smaller numbers also found themselves in operations in South America, Ireland and Burma.

Carnage in the Crimea – 1847-1855

In 1847 Parliament ended life enlistment, limiting service in the army and Marines to 12 years with re-engagement for another twelve, later reduced to nine, to qualify for pension. The Navy also introduced continuous service by an Order in Council of 1853.

20

In 1848 Portsmouth Division moved into Forton Barracks at Gosport, and Woolwich Division into new barracks which had been built for them facing the Common.

In March 1854 Britain and France, coming to the rescue of the dying Turkish Empire, declared war on Russia. The fleet bombarded Odessa and in September laid siege to Sevastopol. Some 400 Marines from the fleet occupied Eupatoria and covered the flanks of the initial landing and after the armies had marched on the city a further 2,000 Marines, and 2,400 seamen landed with 140 guns. The following month the Russians tried to cut off the army from the main British supply port of Balaclava. Taking up their siege positions, known as Marine Heights, twenty-six guns of the RM Artillery covered the charges of both the Heavy and the Light Brigades. In early November 300 Marines under Captain Hopkins took part in the Battle of Inkerman. During this action a party of Marines, which was clearing some caves under Sgt Richards and Cpl Prettyjohns, was attacked. Prettyjohns seized the leading Russian and threw him back, whilst his men hurled heavy stones at the remainder and became involved in close hand-to-hand fighting. It was at this

Lt Dowell and Bdr Wilkinson about to receive their VCs from Queen Victoria

time that the Victoria Cross was instituted and Cpl Prettyjohns became the first of three Royal Marines to be decorated with this coveted award during the Crimean War.

At the same time, on the northern flank of Russia, another British Fleet was in action in the Baltic Sea. After being joined by the French fleet in August they attacked the Russian forts at Bomarsand, which surrendered without a fight. After leaving the Baltic for the winter, they returned the following year and bombarded Sveaborg (Viborg). In one of the minor raids along the coast Lieutenant Dowell won a VC for towing a sinking cutter from under the Russian guns and rescuing the crew.

Marine battalions seized positions to open up the Sea of Azov in 1855 and in June the British and French assaulted Sevastopol.

Bomb ketches with mortars manned by the RMA in the Baltic, 1855

Severe damage was done to the embrasures and parapets of the guns thereby laying the crews open to heavy fire. During a sortie to patch up the damage Bombardier Thomas Wilkinson exposed himself to enemy fire in order to inspire his comrades to repair the shattered defences,. This subsequently earned him the third VC for the Royal Marines.

World-Wide Wars of the 19th Century – 1855-1873

It was also in 1855 that an Order in Council was issued designating the infantry a 'Light Corps', a title prized as an honour and the training being considered *"the best adapted to the nature which the Corps is generally required to perform when employed ashore"*. The two Corps thus became the Royal Marine Artillery, the 'Blue Marines' and the Royal Marine Light Infantry, 'The Red Marines'. A recruit Depot opened at Deal, Kent in 1861.

In the Indian Mutiny, which broke out in 1857, RM detachments were landed from HM Ships and small parties of Marines were in action at Cawnpore and took part in the Relief of Lucknow. At the same time two battalions were formed in England and sent out to the Second China War and these were joined by a third Provisional Battalion, 300 strong under Lt Col Thomas Lemon, from India, where it had been garrisoning Calcutta. They occupied the vast city of Canton in January 1858, which had been the scene of a fierce battle by nearly 200 Marines eighteen months earlier, when they fought to take the city forts one by one. In June 1857 Marines were involved in the Battle of Fatshan Creek and later the 1st & 2nd Marines, by now reinforced, attacked the Taku Forts which guarded the mouth of the Pei-ho river. The marines landed in small boats and had to cross wide mud flats and water filled ditches before reaching the walls. The ranks were cut to ribbons and it is recorded that *"Not 150 men reached the second ditch, and only fifty the third, at the foot of the ramparts. A single scaling ladder was thrown up and a mere ten men tried to force the great fortress. They then withdrew with great difficulty."* The Marines subsequently provided a guard for the naval contingent in Tientsin. When the Taku Forts were taken the following year, the Marines were once again to the fore. They were with the British 1st Division when it entered Peking in 1860. During the Second China War the Marines had lost 232 men killed and 22 wounded.

At the end of 1863, when there was internal strife in Japan, an RMLI Battalion went out to reinforce the Legation Guard at Yokohama where they had been threatened by the Samurai. To carry the battalion HMS *Conqueror* had been converted by the removal of her main deck guns, shades of the Commando ships a century

23

A group of RMLI Officers at Forton Barracks, Gosport c1867

later. The following year they formed part of an allied force that attacked Simonoseki, thus ending the anti-foreign movement in Western Japan. Another battalion went out to Yokohama in 1870 and remained there for five years, being well received not only by the Japanese people, but by the Mikado himself. A battalion serving in Mexico in 1861 even provided a mounted detachment and seven years later Marines from HM Ships were landed with a naval brigade taking a modest part in the Abyssinian expedition.

This was now a time for imperial policing and a period during which the strength of the Corps remained fairly steady. Nevertheless, as an economy measure, after an existence of only 56 years, Woolwich Division was closed in 1869, when officers were placed on half-pay and men forcibly discharged. However in the same year the Depot at Deal was enlarged when North and South Barracks were taken over.

Troubles in Africa and the Far East – 1873-1898

Since the abolition of the slave trade in 1807, the security of British trading settlements on the coast of West Africa had been largely left to the Admiralty, which kept ships off the coast to suppress slavers and pirates. In 1873, when the Ashanti threatened the coast in East Africa, a small mixed contingent of RMA, with two mountain

24

guns and 200 war rockets, plus 110 RMLI, under Lt Col Francis Festing RMA, was sent out in June to restore order. Supported by marines and seamen from the fleet they defeated 2,000 Ashanti, but by the end of July most had gone down with fever and were replaced by 200 Marines from the UK. Later in the year they joined up with a force of three army battalions which, after some jungle skirmishes, forced the Ashanti back into their own territory. RM ships' detachments served ashore with naval brigades in Malaya in 1874/5, in Zanzibar in 1875, the Congo in 1875/6, in Samoa in 1876, on the Niger in 1876/7 and afloat in the constant task of defeating slavery. When Cyprus was ceded to Britain in 1878 seamen and marines occupied the island until a permanent garrison arrived while in the following year Marines from the fleet formed part of the naval brigade during the Zulu War.

War broke out in Egypt in June 1882 when Britain supported the Khedive against the dictator Arabi Pasha; large numbers of the RMA and RMLI were soon involved. Unable to intervene to stop the rioting and murder of Europeans in Alexandria, the Mediterranean Fleet bombarded the batteries and when Arabi Pasha's Egyptian Army withdrew, ships' detachments were formed into a battalion and landed to hold the city and restore order. The arrival of the Channel

The RMLI storming the lines at Tel-el-Kebir, 1882 *from a sketch by Colonel Field*

25

Squadron in July with more Marines, joined in August by another mixed RMA/RMLI battalion, resulted in the seizure of Port Said and Ismailia almost without resistance. The Marines were later reorganised into an RMA and an RMLI Battalion and, with the former serving as infantry, joined General Sir Garnet Wolseley's force preparing to march on Cairo from the Suez Canal, whilst Arabi's attention was fixed on Alexandria. The RMA Battalion soon saw action with an advance force under General Graham at Kassassin and after a night march both battalions were in the dawn attack on the strongly held fortified lines at Tel-el-Kebir, which covered the approaches to Cairo. With the RMLI Battalion being the first to storm the defences, a fierce battle resulted in RMLI losses of 13 killed and 54 wounded, but the Egyptians were routed. The force reached Cairo the following day and on 19th October the two Marine battalions returned to England.

Having put the Khedive back on the throne, the British found themselves faced with the problem of the Sudan where the Mahdi had risen against Egyptian rule. Once more 150 seamen and marines were hastily landed in February 1884, this time from ships at Suakin, before a battalion from the Mediterranean Fleet arrived, to be joined later by another battalion from the UK. They fought actions at El Teb on the Red Sea coast and at Tamai where Osman Digma's 'fuzzy-wuzzies' proved tenacious. At El Teb 380 marines positioned on the left flank carried out a daring flanking movement against the Mahdi's men who were encamped in the hills. Thousands of Dervishes rose up and charged down the hill at the main square of troops, but they were cut down with a loss of 3,000 of their 6,000 men. An RMLI company served with the Guards Camel Regiment in the Desert Column in the attempt to relieve Khartoum. The fierce action at Abu Klea on 17th January 1885 was described by Winston Churchill as *"the most savage action fought by the British troops in the Sudan"*. During the re-conquest of the Sudan in 1896, RMA NCOs trained and supervised Egyptians manning guns in the river gunboats on the Nile, whilst officers from both branches of the Corps were seconded to the Egyptian Army and saw action at the Battle of Omdurman.

An unusual occurrence during this period was the deployment of a detachment on Special Service to Dublin in 1882/3. After the infamous Phoenix Park murders when Lord Frederick Cavendish,

26

the Chief Secretary of Ireland, and others were assassinated, 300 specially selected marines dressed in plain clothes spent six months on policing and guard duties in Ireland.

As this era drew to a close varying numbers of the Corps were in action on the Irrawaddy in Burma, in East and West Africa between 1891 and 1896, in Sierra Leone and Zanzibar in 1896 and even in Crete. During the 1890s Royal Marines battalions were formed each year to train with the army at Aldershot and for several years battalions from Plymouth did so on Dartmoor – shades of things to come. As the pressures of sea service increased and the prospect of action ashore diminished, military training on this scale became subsidiary to the needs of the fleet.

Boers and Boxers – 1899-1902
When the Second Boer War broke out in South Africa in 1899 to meet the demands for field artillery, the Navy brought ships' guns ashore and mounted them on improvised carriages while the RM detachments provided the escorts. The British garrisons of Cape Colony and Natal found themselves heavily outnumbered and out-gunned as the Boers had brought in heavy calibre weapons and the highly mobile Boer commandos proved more than a nuisance. However, the 6-inch naval guns on their makeshift mountings proved more than a match for the Boers. On

The Battle of Graspan *from a painting by Charles Stadden*

27

25th November the RMLI had a chance to show their expertise as an assault force in the Battle of Graspan. After a preliminary bombardment they advanced in extended order across the open veldt under enemy fire. Their losses of 8 killed and 83 wounded out of a total force of 190 Marines were severe as they were such an easy target were they in their tight formation only four paces apart. Over on the east coast another naval brigade was formed from ships at Durban and whilst the naval guns provided artillery support for the advance on Ladysmith the Marines were landed only to provide the infantry defence of the city.

At the end of May 1900, on the other side of the globe the Boxers were threatening the foreign legations in Peking. Included in the international force that was assembled, the RMLI provided three officers and 76 Marines plus three naval ratings and the US Marine Corps two officers and 53 men, the first time the two Corps had fought alongside each other. Besides the British and American legations, there were Russian, German, Italian, Austrian and Japanese missions contained within the small compound adjacent to the Imperial City walls. The force arrived on the 13th and a week later, the Imperial government ordered the legations to leave but, on his way to discuss evacuation, the German minister was murdered by his Chinese escort, and so the siege began. The Chinese established themselves close round the perimeter and made constant forays, burning buildings and shooting at anything that moved.

On 24th June Captain Lewis Halliday RMLI with a section of twenty men was severely wounded when leading a sortie against the Boxer intruders. Despite his wounds he engaged the enemy in hand to hand fighting eventually driving them off. For his gallantry he was awarded the VC, whilst a CGM and five DCMs were awarded to RM NCOs of the Legation detachment. It was from operating so closely together during the 55 days siege in Peking, that today's strong bond between the Royal Marines and the United States Marine Corps was established.

The Corps also took a prominent part in the large international relief force which set out from the mouth of the Peiho River on 9th June. Travelling by rail towards Peking, they were brought to a halt 25 miles from the city where the rails had been torn up. After being

28

Royal Marines manning the 'International' gun at Peking

attacked by Imperialist troops, they staged a withdrawal towards Tientsin. In the early hours of the 21st they came under heavy fire from the Hsuku arsenal, and Major Johnstone led his marines and half a company of seamen back up the road, across the river and made a bayonet attack on the fortress driving the Boxers out. This provided plenty of food and supplies for the beleaguered column. More heavy fighting broke out around Tientsin on 4th August but this was repulsed and the column eventually reached Peking on the 15th, much to the relief of the legation guards.

Chapter 4

Early 20th Century
1902-1939

Q ueen Victoria had appointed her second son, HRH The Prince Alfred, Duke of Edinburgh and Duke of Saxe Coburg-Gotha as Honorary Colonel of the Royal Marines in 1882. He died in 1900 and on 2nd January 1901 HRH The Duke of York, the Prince of Wales' second son, became Colonel-in-Chief of the Royal Marine Forces, a revised title which was much favoured by the Corps and an appointment he continued to hold when he became King George V in 1910. In 1902, as Prince of Wales, he led a brigade of four Marine battalions past his father, King Edward VII, at the Aldershot coronation review. When Queen Victoria died at Osborne House on the Isle of Wight on 22nd January 1901, Royal Marines bands played in the funeral procession, while RMLI sentries from Forton kept watch on the coffin as it lay overnight in the Royal Yacht *Victoria & Albert*. The following day Royal Marines from Forton were formed up as the funeral train steamed slowly past.

    In 1903, the Royal Marines assumed responsibility for

One of the last Royal Naval Bands – HMS *Calcutta*

providing bands in HM Ships and RN shore establishments, and the Royal Naval School of Music was formed at Eastney. Divisional bands had been established at Chatham, Portsmouth, and Plymouth with their own methods of entry, training and engagement but ships' bands had always been found partly by privately engaging musicians for the commission and partly from a small naval band service founded in 1863. Now they would have their own pay, conditions, training and promotion structure leading to commissioned rank as Musical Directors.

The Fisher Reforms of the early years of the century had a disastrous effect on the Corps when, with the naval vote increasing, their numbers were gradually reduced and those who served spent most of their time at sea. Admiral Sir John Fisher was well aware of the under-employment of RM officers afloat, but as he hated the Army, the Navy's rival for public funds, he would not tolerate most RM officers' desire for military training and even employment ashore. He even introduced a scheme whereby all officers for the naval service carried out the same training and cadets appointed to the Marines were commissioned as Lieutenants (M). This was against strong opposition from the Corps and resulted in an acute shortage of junior officers when war broke out in 1914. No doubt if Fisher had been asked 'What are the marines for?' he would have replied that they were there to man the guns of the fleet. This held little truck with the seamen who were now a much more disciplined long-service body, and who excelled at naval gunnery themselves.

The Great War

On the outbreak of hostilities in 1914, the majority of the Corps was serving at sea, but a Royal Marine Brigade was immediately formed largely from reservists and partially trained recruits. The RMA, Chatham, Portsmouth and Plymouth Divisions each provided a battalion and in three weeks this formation was on the other side of the Channel. It was withdrawn after only seven days and the RMA battalion was relieved by one from Deal. It was now realised that Antwerp was the major threat and, after a visit from Winston Churchill, then First Lord of the Admiralty, the Marine

31

Brigade was ordered there on 4th October, but not before 200 men were despatched to Dunkirk to serve with the RN Air Service armoured cars, popularly known as 'The Motor Bandits'. The Brigade was subsequently joined by two naval brigades which had formed up at Walmer; thus creating the nucleus of the famous RN Division. The Antwerp operation was a strategic success, allowing more time for the army to extend its flank northwards. The Division was withdrawn to the UK and reorganised on Army lines, brought up to strength and prepared for service overseas.

Royal Marine Artillery ashore in Belgium in 1914, still wearing blue uniform

On being withdrawn from the RM Brigade the RMA battalion was formed into two Artillery Brigades for service in France, one of super heavy 15-inch howitzers on field mountings, the other of light AA pom-poms. By 1916 there were ten of these heavy howitzers in action and they supported most of the great offensives on the Western Front, playing a particularly important role on the Somme and at Passchendale. Their casualties in the latter action were 35 killed and 97 wounded, in addition to the many who were badly gassed.

Recruiting in 1793 *an engraving by Bunbury*

The First Fleet nearing Australia in 1788 *from a painting by Rex Phillips*

THE EARLY MARINE REGIMENTS 1664-1748

Left to Right – A Grenadier and Ensign, Duke of York and Albany's Maritime Regiment, 1664: Prince George of Denmark's Regiment, 1686: Earl of Torrington's Marines, 1691: Holt's Regiment of Marines, Earl of Donegal's Regiment for Sea Service, Fox's, Villier's and Saunderson's Marines, 1702-1712: 1st, 4th, 2nd and 6th Marines, 1740-1748: Private, Marine Invalid Company, 1740. *A painting by Charles Stadden in the RM Museum*

THE MARINE CORPS AND THE ROYAL MARINES 1755-1807

Left to Right – Sergeant, Drummer and Colour Officer, The Marine Corps, c1758; Officer, Grenadier and Sergeant, Marine Corps Grenadier Company, c1775; Surgeon, Light Company Private, Grenadier and Sergeant, The Marine Corps, 1773-1790; Two Marine Corps Officers, 1798; Sergeant and Drummer, Royal Marines, 1805. *A painting by Charles Stadden in the RM Museum*

34

THE ROYAL MARINES AND THE ROYAL MARINE ARTILLERY 1807-1854

Left to Right – Two Privates RMA, (Blue Undress and Full Dress), 1807; RM Officer, (Full Dress), 1815; Gunner RMA, 1817; RM Officer, (Full Dress), 1823; RM Private, (Drill Order), 1830; Trumpeter RMA and Drummer RM, 1829; Two RM Officers (Undress Frock and Undress Afloat), c1838; RM Bandsman, 1825; RMA Officer, 1848; RM Private (Marching Order) and Bombardier RMA (Undress), 1854.
A painting by Charles Stadden in the RM Museum

THE ROYAL MARINE ARTILLERY AND LIGHT INFANTRY 1854-1900

Left to Right – RM Private (Crimea), 1854, RMLI Private (China), 1859; Two RMA Officers (Mess Dress and Full Dress) c1870; Two RMLI Privates (Ashanti War and Marching Order), c1874; RMLI Officer (Service Dress, Egypt), 1882 and Corporal (Camel Regiment, Sudan), 1885; RMLI Private (Boats Crew), 1896; RMA Gunner (Tropical Drill Order) and Drummer (Undress), 1896; RMLI Private (Greatcoat); RMA Adjutant (Undress) and Bugler (Marching Order), 1900.
A painting by Charles Stadden in the RM Museum

35

THE ROYAL MARINE ARTILLERY AND LIGHT INFANTRY 1900-1923

Left to Right – Gunner RMA (Working Dress), 1916; RMLI Marching Order, Corporal 1900 and Private 1917; RMLI Officers, (Mess Dress 1900 and Review Order 1908); RMA Musician, 1910; RMA Officers, (Review Order 1900, Undress 1922 and Mess Dress 1900); RMLI Drummer (Review Order), 1922; RMLI Officer (Drill Order), 1904; RMA Field Officer (Drill Order), 1914; RMA Gunner (SW Africa) 1917; RMLI SNCO (Tropical Review Order) 1900. *A painting by Charles Stadden in the RM Museum*

THE ROYAL MARINES 1923-1946

Left to Right – Colonel Commandant (Review Order), 1928; Field Officer (Mess Dress), 1939; Officer (Battle Dress), 1941; Marine (Embarkation Order), 1938; Marine (Khaki Drill Review Order), 1939; Colour Sergeant (Review Order), 1935; Marine (NW Europe Commando), 1944; QMSI (First Drill) (Drill Order), 1939; Recruit (Khaki, Drill Order), 1939; Corporal (RM Provost Company), 1943; Marine (Blue Battledress, Boats Crew), 1944; Marine (Far East Commando), 1945; Musician (RM Divisional Band Review Order), 1935; General Officer (Review Order), 1936. *A painting by Charles Stadden in the RM Museum*

36

THE ROYAL MARINES 1946-1973

Left to Right – Marine (Malaya), 1951; Corporal (Southern Arabia), 1964; Officer (Khaki Service Dress), 1946; RSM (No. 1 Dress), 1969; Corporal (Lovat Dress), 1969; Colour Sergeant (Greatcoat), 1948; SNCO (Tropical Mess Dress), 1959; Musician (Tropical Dress), 1959; Officer (Khaki Drill), 1960; Adjutant (Blue Uniform), 1956; Bugler (Ceremonial), 1969, Officer (Red Sea Rig), 1959; General Officer (Ceremonial), 1964; Marine (Combat Dress), 1969. *A painting by Charles Stadden in the RM Museum*

THE ROYAL MARINES 1973

Left to Right – Corporal (Barrack Working Dress); Sergeant (Lovat Dress – RM Raincoat); Cook; Musician (Ceremonial Dress – Blue Band Cape); Warrant Officer 2 (Mess Dress); Despatch Rider; Marine (Naval Working Dress); Swimmer Canoeist; Cold Weather Warfare Dress; Sergeant Pilot; Physical Training Instructor (PT Sweater); Staff Physical Training Instructor (PT Vest); Sniper; Drum Major (Ceremonial Dress). *A painting by Charles Stadden in the RM Museum*

The Cutting Out of *"La Chevrette"*, 1801
from a painting in Bristol City Art Gallery by de Loutherberg.

While inspecting the guard aboard *Bellerophon*, Napoleon remarked that much might be done with 100,000 men such as these! *from a painting by Captain Hicks*

The Battle of Hernani during the Carlist War, 1837 *from a painting by Cunliffe*

A Royal Marine Artillery field battery on Southsea Common, c1843
from a painting by Cunliffe

The RMLI provided a Company for the Guards Camel Regiment.
"A Halt in the Bayuda Desert" 1885 *from a painting by Bartelli*

Royal Marines landing from HMS *Vindictive* at Zeebrugge, 1918 *from a painting by de Lacy*

Gallipoli

In January 1915 when Turkey entered the war on the side of the Central Powers a decision was made to open up the Dardanelles by a naval attack. After the first bombardments protection for naval demolition parties was provided by RM detachments landed from two of the bombarding battleships. The first elements of the RM Brigade, the Chatham and Plymouth Battalions had already sailed for the Eastern Mediterranean in February. The first to land were two companies of the Plymouth Battalion, also as protection for demolition parties, one company went ashore at Sedd-el-Bahr and the other at Kum Kale on the other side of the Dardanelles, thereby operating against the Turks on two continents simultaneously. Their tasks mainly accomplished after meeting strong opposition, they were able to re-embark in good order. The main contribution from the Corps came later in the form of the Royal Naval Division under the command of an RMA General, (later Sir) Archibald Paris, which, with the 29th Division landed on the southernmost tip of the Gallipoli Peninsula. The Corps provided No 3 Brigade with the Chatham, Portsmouth and Plymouth Battalions, while the Deal Battalion was in No 1 Brigade, commanded by Brig Gen D Mercer with the Drake and Nelson Battalions of seamen.

The Gallipoli Beaches, 1915

41

On 25th April Plymouth Battalion RMLI landed on 'Y' Beach on the left flank, were in action for 30 hours and took heavy casualties from a Turkish counter-attack.

Three days later the Chatham and Portsmouth Battalions landed at Anzac beach and took over the centre of the line, being joined two days later by Deal and Nelson battalions. It was during the fierce fighting here that L/Cpl W R Parker, a stretcher-bearer, was taking supplies to forward positions across open ground which was being swept by machine gun fire. Despite most of his companions being killed, he pressed on and assisted the wounded in the forward trenches to safety. For this selfless action he was awarded the VC. As the campaign developed into a stalemate the freezing blizzards, severe frostbite and flooded trenches during the winter took their toll and casualties mounted. The losses in the four Marine Battalions were so great that the remnants of Chatham and Deal were amalgamated into the 1st Battalion RMLI and those of Portsmouth and Plymouth into the 2nd RMLI. Troops were gradually withdrawn and the 2nd Battalion were the final troops to leave giving rise to the maxim 'First in, last out'. The RM casualties at Gallipoli were over 100 officers and 3,000 NCOs and men killed or wounded.

The Western Front

From Gallipoli the Division moved to the Western Front and arriving in France it was re-equipped and reorganised. Together with the Howe and Anson Naval Battalions, the two RMLI Battalions formed the 188th Infantry Brigade of the renamed 63rd (Royal Naval) Division. In addition to the two battalions, the Corps provided the Divisional Machine Gun Battalion and RMLI officers commanded some of the naval battalions, whilst others were company commanders.

At Passchendale, on one day, the RMLI lost 680 men killed, wounded or missing out of a total of 1,170. By 1918 their losses were so severe that the battalions were reduced to one and the 1st Battalion RMLI ended the war in the pursuit to Mons. The Royal Marine Artillery, providing a Howitzer Brigade and an AA Brigade, were engaged in almost every action on the Western Front from Aubers in 1915 onwards, including the Somme, Ancre, Ypres, Passchendale, Cambrai, Arras and many others.

A 15" Howitzer of the RMA in action on the Western Front, 1917

The fighting done by a tiny minority of the Corps, to whit the RMLI Battalions and the RMA on the Western Front was far more than the rest of the Royal Marines in the whole war. The only Victoria Cross awarded to the Corps on the Western Front was to Major F W Lumsden RMA, whilst commanding an army battalion in France in 1917. He was killed a year later in the front line when commanding a Brigade soon after adding a third bar to the DSOs he had won in 1917. He was also appointed CB in the King's Birthday Honours for 1918. A memorial to him stands in the Royal Marines Museum Garden of Remembrance at Eastney

At sea the Marines were also engaging the Germans. On 31st May 1916, some 132 officers and warrant officers and 5,700 NCOs and men were present at the major naval engagement of the war, the Battle of Jutland. Manning turrets in most of the capital ships they kept the guns firing. In the battle cruiser HMS *Lion*, flagship of Admiral Beatty, an 11-inch shell hit 'Q' turret, manned by marines, blowing open the roof and killing most of the gun's crew. Major Harvey RMLI, having lost both legs, gave the order to flood the magazine thus ensuring that the fire did not spread below to the magazine and blow up the ship. He was awarded a posthumous VC, but 50 Royal Marines in the ship were killed in the action. However the highest proportion of Royal Marines decorated from one ship at Jutland was to HMS *Chester*, where the OCRM Captain Edward Bamford was awarded the DSO and five of his 40 marines were also rewarded.

Zeebrugge

"I am confident that the great traditions of our forefathers will be worthily maintained, and that all ranks will strive to emulate the heroic deeds of our brothers in France and Flanders" concluded the message Vice Admiral Roger Keyes sent to the officers and men taking part in the gallant raid on Zeebrugge in 1918. The task was to stop the U-boats that were based on the Bruges canals from putting to sea. The 4th Battalion Royal Marines, quickly reorganised in Deal with a cover story that they were training for a raid in France with the Royal Naval Division. After a fortnight's training and waiting for the right conditions, the force sailed on the moonlit night of 22nd April. As it left, Keyes signalled *"St George for England"* to which Captain Carpenter in HMS *Vindictive* replied *"May we give the dragon's tail a damned good twist!"*

The plan was to block the canal entrances with three obsolete cruisers and the job of the *Vindictive*, along with the requisitioned Liverpool ferryboats *Iris* and *Daffodil*, was to carry the storming parties. Marines and sailors under Lieutenant Colonel Elliot and Captain Halahan RN were to silence the gun batteries on the Zeebrugge mole that protected the harbour while the blockships were scuttled. The approach was made under cover of drizzle and an elaborate smoke screen, but a sudden breeze blew the smoke away when the *Vindictive* was about 400 yards off and the attackers were met with the full force of the enemy guns on the mole. Elliot and Halahan were both killed but the attack went in with the troops storming across the remaining two specially constructed wooden brows or gangplanks. They berthed 300 yards further on from their planned position and then had to drop down 16 feet from the top of the wall to the main level of the mole, all under heavy fire. The German guns were particularly aimed at the foretop positions in the ship where marines were manning the guns. Sergeant N A Finch

The brows aboard *Vindictive* constructed for landing on the Zeebrugge Mole

RMA was one of these and despite all around him being killed or wounded, he continued to work his Lewis gun. Meanwhile Capt E Bamford RMLI, who had already won a DSO in HMS *Chester* at the Battle of Jutland, led Portsmouth Company along the mole *"displaying the greatest initiative in the command of his company and a complete disregard of danger"* and took the German strong point before assaulting the battery. After an hour the remnants of the attackers, taking their wounded with them, re-embarked and returned to England. Two Victoria Crosses were awarded to the 4th Battalion to be balloted for under the 9th Statute of the Order and these went to Bamford and Finch. As a mark of respect it was decreed that no future RM battalion would ever be numbered 4th.

When he visited the 4th Battalion at Deal on 7th March 1918 before they sailed for Zeebrugge, King George V also witnessed recruit training. He decreed that the senior recruit squad under training should henceforth be known as the King's Squad and the best all-round recruit should be awarded the King's Badge, providing he reached a sufficiently high standard *(see Appendix H)*.

Other World War 1 Activities

Royal Marine Engineers, specially raised for the war, constructed camps and installations for the Royal Navy and towards the end of hostilities there was even an RM Labour Corps working the Channel Ports. In South Africa in 1916 Royal Marines trained members of the Union Defence Force and subsequently fought through the East African campaigns of 1916 and 1917.

Russia 1918-1919 and Expeditions to Ireland and Chanak

An ad hoc Royal Marines Field Force had been sent to Murmansk in July 1918 and was deployed along the 300 miles of railway from there to Kem on the White Sea. Further east in 1919, thirty Royal Marines volunteers and some sailors, under the command of Captain Thomas Jameson, from HMS *Suffolk* and *Kent* travelled 6,000 miles from Vladivostock across Siberia to support the Russian White Army. After transporting one 6-inch gun and four 12 pounder guns on railway trucks, they mounted the large gun on to a paddle driven tug and took part in operations on the Kama River, a tributary of the Volga.

Royal Marines with the 6" gun they transported by rail across Siberia in 1919

The Field Force was relieved by the 6th Battal
proved an unhappy time when the greater part of two
mutinied. After a court martial 1 officer was dismissed
1 NCO and 12 men were sentenced to death for 'wilfu
which was later commuted to 5 years penal servitude, while 73 others
were sentenced to various other punishments.

The 8th Battalion spent two years in Southern Ireland
arriving there in June 1920 to guard coastal installations during early
Sinn Fein troubles. There was a happier outcome to the 11 Battalion's
tour to Constantinople where they arrived on 2nd October 1922
deploying alongside the army, all protecting the city and covering
the Chanak bridgehead, which held open the Dardanelles' sea
route. They withdrew after a year.

Amalgamation in 1923

The amalgamation of the Royal Marine Artillery and the
Royal Marine Light Infantry into a single Corps had been under con-
sideration since the end of the Great War, when demobilisation
reduced the Corps strength from 55,000 to 15,000. By 1922, the
Treasury, after trying to abolish the Royal Marines, reduced their
number to 9,500 on the understanding that one Division was given
up. Forton Barracks at Gosport was closed and Eastney Barracks,
completed in 1864 to house the RMA, was retained to become the
home of the Portsmouth Division Royal Marines.

The amalgamation decision was announced by an Admiralty
Fleet Order of June 1923 and the ranks of Gunner and Private were
replaced by that of Marine. A cadre of officers and NCOs would
continue to be trained at the School of Land Artillery in Fort
Cumberland, but otherwise the training of the Corps would be as
infantrymen and seaman gunners, with Deal chosen as the centralised
recruit training establishment. The Corps needed a new role and
the official instructions read:

*"Its function in war and peace is to provide detachments which,
whilst fully capable of manning their share of the gun armament
of ships, are specially trained to provide a striking force, drawn
either from the Divisions or from the Fleet, immediately
available for use under the direction of the Commander-in-*

47

Chief for amphibious operations such as raids on the enemy coastline and bases, or the seizure and defence of temporary bases for the use of our own Fleet."

In January 1927 when the Chinese Nationalist armies were marching on Shanghai the 12th Battalion was hastily formed and sailed within a week. They formed part of the Shanghai Defence Force to guard the international settlements, and when the tension eased in December, they were withdrawn to England.

Ranks of the 12th RM Battalion embarking for service in Shanghai, 1927

In 1935, Italy invaded Abyssinia and in view of the threat of war, 1,600 Marines were sent out to Egypt to set up defences at Alexandria, where they provided coast artillery as well as manning anti-aircraft guns and searchlights. All the men returned to the UK in July 1936. This was the forerunner of the two Mobile Naval Base Defence Organisations (MNBDO) that were subsequently raised with a huge investment in men and equipment for the forthcoming war. On return to England a nucleus was retained at Fort Cumberland where pier-building equipment and the Landing Craft Mechanized were developed. Although the amphibious concept might seem to be taking

The early days of landing craft in Langstone Harbour Portsmouth, 1929

shape it still lagged badly, not least in the Admiralty, where in 1938 the First Sea Lord said that he did not foresee a combined operation being mounted in the next war! The Americans had a different view and were well ahead of Britain in amphibious matters when war broke out.

Transport being landed from one of HM ships during an exercise in the 1930's

An RM Battalion carried out ceremonial duties in London for the first time in 1935

The only visit King Edward VIII paid to the Corps during his short reign was to Eastney in 1936, with Commander Lord Louis Mountbatten as his ADC

Also in 1935, Silver Jubilee year, the Royal Marines carried out ceremonial duties in London for the first time, when a specially formed battalion mounted guard on Buckingham Palace, St James's and on other places of note. Before leaving London, they were able to exercise the privilege of marching through the City with bayonets fixed, drums beating and Colours flying for the first time. They also participated in the other Jubilee ceremonies and two years later in the Coronation of King George VI, keeping the Corps in the public eye at a time when morale was suffering.

Royal Marines officers had taken to the skies before the Great War and were among the first pilots to be trained for the Royal Naval Air Service. Indeed Lt E L Gerrard became an airship pilot in 1909 and two years later was one of the first four officers to train as naval pilots. During World War One 15 pilots and 3 observers flew with the RNAS. There were about 20 pilots during the 1920s but blocked promotion prospects caused the numbers to drop to half a dozen during the 1930s. Just prior to World War Two expansion of the Fleet Air Arm attracted more Royal Marines volunteers as the number of aircraft carriers grew.

A flight of aircraft from HMS *Glorious*, all with RM pilots, over Malta in 1931

51

Chapter 5

Second World War
1939-1945

In 1939 most of the Corps were once again serving at sea when war with Germany broke out. The strength of the Royal Marines was 12,390 with a further 1,082 in the Royal Fleet Reserve. A skeleton organisation was already in being to provide defences for naval bases and this was expanded with reservists and conscripts providing most of the men. From this the RM Fortress Unit was quickly mobilised and sent to Scapa Flow. RM Engineers were formed again and carried out construction work in naval shore establishments and a Siege Regiment, equipped with 14-inch and 13.5-inch guns, was formed to bombard the French coast from railway sidings around the Dover area. By the end of the year, Royal Marines had also been in action at sea, particularly in the Battle of the River Plate.

When the Germans invaded Norway in April 1940 some of the first ashore were marines from HMS *Glasgow* and *Sheffield,*

landing at Namsos and working with the Norwegian Army. Marines from HMS *Nelson, Hood* and *Barham* followed, landing at Andalsnes and Alesund to set up coastal defences while the Fortress Unit went to Northern Norway. Some small ad hoc parties were sent across the Channel, covering the departure of the Queen of the Netherlands from the Hook of Holland and the final withdrawal from Boulogne and Calais. Elements of MNBDO1 were widely

A sketch by Sir Muirhead Bone of one of the 13.5" guns of the RM Siege Regiment, 1942

deployed along the south east coast during the Battle of Britain and the 1st Heavy Anti-Aircraft Regiment registered a record score, accounting for 98 enemy aircraft.

In August the newly formed RM Brigade was despatched to Dakar in an ill-fated operation aimed at persuading the Vichy French to join the Allies but it never landed. Shortly after returning it provided the basis on which a Royal Marine Division was assembled. Although the formation was chosen for a number of operations these never materialized.

The RM band of HMS *Hood* playing on deck. All 17
of the band were lost when the ship was sunk in 1941

During 1941 Marines were constantly in action at sea, on convoy work, in the battles of Crete and Cape Matapan and in the *Bismark* action where the whole detachment of 164 Marines, including the band were lost when HMS *Hood* was sunk. The focus of the war then shifted to the Mediterranean and in January 1941 it was decided to send the MNBDO to the Middle East. After a journey around the Cape and through the Suez Canal, the formation was ordered to Crete but only about half reached the island a few days before the evacuation of Greece began in April. Defences were set up, but when German paratroops landed on 20th May, the Marines, fighting as infantry, were embroiled in the bloody battle and subsequent withdrawal. More than 1,200 Marines were taken prisoner but Major Ralph Garrett and 137 volunteers from the Marines and the army refloated a derelict landing craft and, under improvised sail, managed to reach Egypt. A second MNBDO was raised in England.

A sketch of Major Garrett arriving in North Africa with other survivors who escaped from Crete in a landing craft, 1941

Refitted after Crete MNBDO1, redeployed eastwards in September and set up their guns in Diego Garcia, the Seychelles and at Addu Atoll in the Indian Ocean. When war with Japan broke out in December 1941, one of the first actions was the sinking of HMS *Prince of Wales* and *Repulse*. A large proportion of the crews survived and Marines from the detachments joined up with the 2nd Bn Argyll & Sutherland Highlanders, who had been reduced to 250 men after the fighting in Malaya. Together they formed a battalion and fought in the final stages before the fall of Singapore, inevitably as both ships were from Plymouth, as 'the Plymouth Argylls'. Those who survived were forced to surrender and spent the remainder of the war as prisoners of the Japanese. A further 40 members of the RM detachments died as a result of the privations they endured working on the infamous 'railway of death'.

54

A pier constructed by Royal Marines to enable stores
to be landed for the defence of the Seychelles, 1942

Early in 1942 four officers and 103 volunteers from the Coast Regiment of MNBDO1 went to Rangoon. As Force 'Viper' they were the last to leave the city and, manning motor launches were involved in heavy fighting, whilst covering the withdrawal up the River Irrawaddy. They finally abandoned and destroyed their craft before marching over the mountains into India. In Colombo and Trincomalee the Air Defence Brigade of MNBDO1 were in action when aircraft from the Japanese Fleet attacked Ceylon, while further south Maj-Gen Sturges with a skeleton HQ from the RM Division and two army brigades seized Diego Suarez on Madagascar. When one of the Brigades was held up on the approaches to Antsirane, the RM detachment of HMS *Ramillies* landed from a destroyer and captured the town.

Motor launches manned by Force Viper, for operations on the Irrawaddy in Burma, 1942

Birth of Commandos

Winston Churchill had ordered the establishment of raiding forces soon after the fall of France and the army formed their first Commando in the summer of 1940. The first Royal Marine Commando was formed in 1942 as The Royal Marine Commando and took part in the abortive Dieppe raid on 19th August that year. It became 'A' RM Commando later in the year when 'B' Commando was formed from the 8th Battalion in October. Nevertheless there was some concerted feeling in the higher echelons of the Corps that the RM Division should still be retained, but it soon became apparent that the battalions were not being fully employed and the commando role was exactly what the Corps was all about.

Although the MNBDO cadre had been the first to develop landing craft before the war, little was done in the intervening years. The Admiralty now had an urgent need to man the large number of landing craft that would be required for the assault on mainland Europe. The appointment of Admiral Lord Mountbatten as Chief of Combined Operations, with his foresight and initiative, suggested that this, together with the formation of Commandos, were prime roles for the Royal Marines. With the help of a number of particularly influential leaders, he was able to bring about a reorganisation that changed the face of the Corps.

Landing Craft Flak had an RM detachment of 2 officers and
48 other ranks to man the 2 pdr pom-poms and Oerlikon AA Guns

By January 1943 only one of the three major land formations in which the Corps were involved had seen any action and so the two MNBDOs returned to UK and disbanded. Although the AA regiments were retained and formed into an AA Brigade, most of the remaining ranks were re-trained for service with Combined Operations. The RM Division was also disbanded, and the battalions re-trained at Achnacarry for the commando role. Some of the remaining units were reformed into specialist units in which Royal Marines personnel were particularly suited and others were disbanded and the men also retrained for service with Combined Operations. The Corps was now being prepared for numerous active service roles in the invasion of Europe.

A new secret organisation with the misleading title of Royal Marine Boom Patrol Detachment had been formed at Eastney. In December 1942 Major 'Blondie' Hasler led a team of twelve canoeists to place limpet mines on German blockade runners lying up the Gironde river at Bordeaux. Five canoes, ten men, were launched by submarine and only one crew, Hasler and Marine Sparks, eventually escaped, the remainder being either killed during the raid or executed by the Germans under Hitler's orders. This was the forerunner of the present Special Boat Service, although the army had started such an organisation earlier in the war in the Mediterranean, which had included a few Marines.

57

Royal Marines Aviators

In the air, Royal Marines pilots had taken part in a number of engagements from aircraft carriers, in the Norwegian campaign, in the Battle of Britain, at Matapan and Taranto, afterwards in support of the Sicily landings and later on D-Day and in the Pacific. Five DSOs, nine DSCs and nine Mentions in Despatches were awarded to RM pilots for their bravery.

Thirty-one pilots and two observers saw action with the Fleet Air Arm in World War 2, eighteen of whom eventually commanded squadrons or wings and eight became Commanders (Flying) in aircraft carriers. They particularly distinguished themselves in command appointments culminating with Lt Col Ronnie Hay who became the Air Group Co-ordinator commanding all 218 carrier-borne aircraft in the British Pacific Fleet. Nine former NCOs transferred to the Navy as rating pilots.

The Mediterranean

As more marines were trained the Royal Marines Commandos increased and they were numbered from 40 to 48(RM) Commandos, whilst the army had Nos 1 to 12 Commandos. 40 & 41 Commandos took part on the left flank of the allied landings in Sicily on 10th July 1943 and in the assault on Salerno on 9th September. 41 Commando

Ranks of 43(RM) Commando enjoy a 'brew-up' before the Battle of Comacchio, 1945

58

was involved in seizing the Vietri Pass leading towards Naples. 40 Commando took Termoli on 2nd October, opening up the road north and then went into the line on the Garigliano. On 20th January 1944, 43 Commando landed on the Anzio beachhead where the Germans put up very strong resistance

In March a depleted 40 Commando and later 43 Commando were withdrawn from Italy and joined HQ 2 Special Service Brigade on the island of Vis in the Adriatic. Here they supported Tito's partisans in raids along the Yugoslav coast. A year later 43 Commando returned to the Italian mainland and it was on 3rd April 1945 that Cpl Tom Hunter posthumously won the Corps only VC of World War 2, leading a determined assault on an enemy position near Lake Comacchio.

North-West Europe

In Operation *Overlord*, the invasion of the Continent on 6th June 1944, the Royal Marines made their greatest single contribution to

The RM Armoured Support Group manned
Centaur Tanks for close support in Normandy, 1944

59

the Second World War. In all some 17,500 Marines took part in the landings with four RM Commandos involved in the initial assault 41, 45, 47, 48, and with 46 Commando landing on D+1. 47 Commando's action to capture Port-en-Bessin on D+1 after a ten mile march beyond our own lines and replacing many of their weapons lost in the sea with German ones, was amongst the fiercest. Royal Marines also manned Centaur tanks in an Armoured Support Group of two regiments, which covered the initial landings. At sea the Corps manned two thirds of the assault landing craft, as well as serving in naval beach parties and obstruction clearance units. Nearly all the bombarding ships had Marines manning part of the main and secondary armament.

All five Commandos then took part in subsequent operations through France, Belgium and Holland. On 1st November 41, 47 & 48 Commandos landed at Westkapelle on the tip of Walcheren in the drive to secure the Scheldt with minor landing craft crewed by Royal Marines and manning the guns in the craft of the Support Squadron. The support craft drew the fire of the German shore batteries from the assault craft and consequently suffered very heavy casualties.

47(RM) Commando embarking in LCTs for the Assault on Walcheren, 1944

During 1st SS Brigade's drive across Europe 45 Commando were involved in a bitter battle at Montforterbeek on 23rd January 1945 where L/Cpl Harden RAMC, one of the unit's medical orderlies, won the VC. 45 & 46 Commandos were both involved in crossing the Rhine, Weser, Aller and Elbe rivers, finishing the war at Lubeck on the Baltic coast.. The 5th RM AA Brigade was responsible for the air defence of the port of Antwerp. To meet the army's infantry shortage, two RM infantry brigades were formed in UK from landing craft crews, now surplus to requirements and in February 116 Brigade crossed the river Maas to enter Germany. 117 Brigade did not arrive in Europe until after VE Day and was only involved in the surrender of the German ports.

The Far East

Out in the Far East Marines from the East Indies Fleet seized the island of Cheduba in Burma in January 1944 and 3 SS Brigade, with 5 & 44 Commandos took part in the Arakan campaign in March. They were later joined by Nos 1 and 42 Commando and then in January 1945, when the Japanese were in full retreat, the Brigade, now redesignated 3rd Commando Brigade and under the command of Brig C R Hardy, was sent to cut their escape route. 42 and 44 Commandos were involved in heavy fighting in the mangrove swamps around Kangaw. Having seized hill positions they were subjected to continuous artillery fire. In spite of their heavy casualties, for thirty-six hours the Commandos beat off the repeated counter attacks of the fanatical Japanese until the latter finally withdrew. In a Special Order of the Day General Sir Philip Christianson wrote *"the Battle of Kangaw has been the decisive battle of the whole Arakan campaign"*.

As the war in the Far East ended in August 1945, Royal Marines were preparing for the invasion of Malaya, Operation *Zipper*, both as Commandos and landing craft crews. Force ROMA was hastily formed from Marines of the Far East Fleet to take the surrender in Penang, while 3 Commando Brigade was diverted to Hong Kong where it arrived in early September to assist in the liberation of the Colony. An Amphibian Support Regiment equipped with tracked amphibious vehicles had been formed in the UK to provide close support in the landings envisaged in operations along the coasts of Malaya, Indo-China and Thailand. It arrived in India shortly before VJ Day and was soon carrying out internal security duties as infantry in India and the Dutch East Indies.

By the end of the war the strength of the Corps had reached over 74,000. 3,983 Royal Marines had died during the war, including 225 musicians, a quarter of their strength, and the highest percentage of any branch of any Service. There was a reduction to peace-time strength, the principal roles of the Royal Marines changed and with that came a major reorganisation.

Force ROMA, hastily formed from RM detachments of the
East Indies Fleet, land in Penang to take the Japanese surrender, 1945

Chapter 6

Reorganisation and Deployments
1945-1951

Within two years of the end of the Second World War the numbers had reduced to 13,000 of whom 2,200 were in 3rd Commando Brigade in the Far East and less than 2,000 in the traditional pre-war role at sea. The functions of the Royal Marines now changed with the Corps becoming the leader in many aspects of 'amphibiosity' and exclusively assuming the Commando role, whilst still providing detachments and bands for HM Ships, albeit a dwindling task.

As regulars replaced 'hostilities only' men in commandos, the numerical designations of the Commandos were chosen to represent the three theatres of war in which they had fought. 40 Commando was disbanded in the UK, but 44 Commando was renumbered '40'

Above The Commando Memorial above Spean Bridge, unveiled in 1952.
Left The RM Commando Memorial, Lympstone, unveiled in 1986.

and represented the Mediterranean theatre, 42 Commando the Far East and 45 Commando North-West Europe.

The Harwell committee, set up to examine the structure of the peace time services, recommended the abolition of the Corps, but fortunately the Admiralty did not agree although they insisted that the strength should be proportionate to that of the Royal Navy at 10%. At the top General Sir Thomas Hunton changed his title, first to General Officer Commanding Royal Marines and then to Commandant General Royal Marines with direct access to the Admiralty Board. The Corps was streamlined in the next few years with the administrative Divisions becoming functional Groups; centralised pay, records and drafting; the formation of the RM Commando School, firstly at Towyn in North Wales and then Bickleigh in 1947; the Depot at Exton became the Infantry Training Centre; and the Royal Marine Forces Volunteer Reserve (now the Royal Marines Reserve), similar to the Territorial Army, initially of 200 officers and 1,300 other ranks was formed in 1948.

In order to achieve the reduction in the strength of the Corps, pressure was exerted on the Commandant General to disband the Commando Brigade, but in 1950 General Sir Leslie Hollis persuaded the Board of Admiralty that this could be accomplished by closing Chatham Group. In the summer of that year the massed bands of the Royal Marines Beat Retreat on Horse Guards Parade in London for the first time, an event which was later to be repeated at regular intervals in the ceremonial calendar of the Corps. This came to be seen as a precursor to the amalgamation of the bands formed from the Royal Naval School of Music and the old Divisional bands, to form the Royal Marines School of Music at Deal later in the year and the appointment of its first Principal Director of Music, Lieutenant Colonel F Vivian Dunn.

By 1950 the Special Boat Company (later Squadron, and now Service) had become an all Royal Marines unit of a headquarters and six sections (one at Eastney, two in the Rhine Squadron, one with 3rd Commando Brigade and two from the RMFVR), emanating from a variety of amphibious special forces units formed during the war.

So the Corps began to take on a new shape. Operationally it was fully employed with 3rd Commando Brigade moving from Hong

Kong to Malta in 1946. 40 Commando was soon involved in the Israeli/Palestinian unrest and two years later with 42 and 45 Commandos in the withdrawal from Palestine, 40 Commando being the last to leave. All three Commandos spent time in Egypt guarding lines of communications in the Canal Zone including the security of the Suez Canal. 45 Commando was sent to Akaba in Transjordan in 1949 when trouble threatened. One Commando was usually stationed in Cyprus. There is little doubt that the continued deployments of the Commando Brigade in keeping the peace around the world during this time helped the Admiralty change its mind about abolishing it. For the first time it became an affordable asset to the senior service.

Meanwhile at home His Majesty King George VI, who had succeeded to the title of Colonel-in-Chief on coming to the throne in 1937, changed his title to Captain General and soon afterwards dined with more than 300 Royal Marines officers at the Savoy Hotel in London on 21st December 1949.

Far East Unrest

In July 1949, Communist China threatened the sovereignty of Hong Kong, by massing on its border. 3 Commando Brigade was sent there, sailing together in the SS *Georgic*, with HQ, 40 & 42 Commandos embarking in Malta and picking up 45 Commando from Port Suez. For the next eight months they provided the internal security for Hong Kong and the hundreds of outlying islands.

In May 1950 the whole Brigade left Hong Kong for a tour of duty in the long drawn out Malayan Emergency. This was probably the most critical period of the whole campaign when violence reached its peak. The Chinese Communists, from bases deep in the jungle, were engaged in infiltrating Chinese and Malay villages, in terrorising the locals, arson, murder and other anti-colonial activities in an attempt to win over the hearts and minds of the people. 3 Commando Brigade was tasked with counter-insurgency warfare in support of the civil administration and police. In the northern state of Perak, the Brigade had a responsibility for an area the size of Wales. The Headquarters and 42 Commando were initially based in Ipoh; 40 Commando in Taiping were given the Thailand border areas of Grik and Kroh; 45 Commando had an equally vast area centred

A patrol of 45 Commando crossing a river during the Malayan emergency, 1951.

on Tapah from the Cameron Highlands in the east to the coastal plain in the west. In the next two years all three units were continually involved in jungle fighting and counter terrorist activity. During this time they killed 171 terrorists and captured more than 50. The Commander-in-Chief, General Sir John Harding, later described it as *"a record of hard work, devotion to duty and good comradeship of which the Royal Marines have every reason to be proud"*. The Corps lost 30 killed in the campaign and won 40 gallantry awards, not including 'mentions in despatches'.

Meanwhile North Korean troops had crossed the 38th parallel into South Korea on 25th June 1950 and a United Nations force was raised. In August a small force of volunteers from the British Far East Fleet was placed at the disposal of the US Navy to raid coastal communications, and the following month the Commandant General was tasked with raising a special unit for this purpose. In early September 41 Independent Commando, some 200 strong (later 300) left UK for Japan under Lt Col Douglas Drysdale. They made three successful raids behind enemy lines cutting railway lines along the north-eastern coast of Korea. During October the Americans and South Koreans followed up a defeated enemy across the border as far as Hungnam. When the Chinese attacked this

force and cut the supply route between the Chosin reservoir and Hungnam, 41 Commando were sent to join the 1st US Marine Division and soon given the task of escorting 100 relief lorries through enemy lines to Hagaru-Ri. Supported by 29 tanks of the US Marine Corps, they fought their way overnight along the hill features guarding the ten-mile route against heavy opposition. In atrocious arctic conditions they finally reached Hagaru-Ri and joined up

A raiding party of 41 Independent Commando preparing to demolish a railway line, Korea, 1951.

with 1st Marine Division in defensive positions. After regrouping and retraining in Japan, 41 Commando landed on the north-eastern coast, 150 miles behind enemy lines on 7 April 1951. They remained ashore eight hours to demolish the railway line. In July they established a base on Wonsan Island 60 miles inside enemy territory from where they made a number of raids.

The unit was recalled to England at the end of 1951 being disbanded the following February. They had lost 31 killed including three RN medical staff while 29 were taken prisoner 10 of whom died in captivity. 18 officers and men were decorated apart from 10 'mentions' and 13 US awards. For their part in the epic breakout at Hagaru-Ri 41 Commando was subsequently awarded the high honour of a Presidential Unit Citation, which was later borne on their Regimental Colour to be paraded once a year. During the Korean War Royal Marines detachments at sea were also engaged in many bombardment actions and a number of officers saw action as Fleet Air Arm pilots.

Chapter 7

More Brush Fire Wars
1952-1970

In May 1952 the Brigade returned to Malta from Malaya and in November the units received their first Colours from HRH The Duke of Edinburgh on Floriana Parade Ground, Valetta. Including Marines from the fleet and landing craft who kept the ground, there were 67 officers and 1,168 men on parade. In his address, Prince Philip, who was appointed Captain General the following year, said *"These Colours are a recognition of the devotion of the wartime Royal Marines Commandos and of the courage and bearing of the Brigade in all the trouble spots of the world since the war"*.

Although Royal Marines Commandos did not serve with the British Army of the Rhine, the Corps had a landing craft presence on the Rhine during the 1950s, when Royal Marines manned craft in the Rhine Squadron, but this was withdrawn from Germany in 1958.

It was not long before there was further unrest in the Suez Canal Zone and the whole Brigade, including the Headquarters, was sent there in May 1953 to carry out internal security duties, during which they were frequently sniped at by dissident Egyptians. The Brigade returned to Malta late in 1954, with 42 Commando continuing on to the UK to take over Commando Training at Bickleigh. In Cyprus EOKA terrorists, claiming a union with Greece, were now causing trouble. In September 1955, at 48 hours notice, Brigade HQ, 40 and 45 Commandos were hastily embarked in HM Ships as part of a build up of troops sent to the island to combat the serious disturbances. In August 1956 President Nasser of Egypt nationalised the Suez Canal. Once again the Brigade moved at short notice in HM Ships, this time to concentrate back in Malta. Meanwhile the operational nucleus of 42 Commando was quickly brought up to strength and went out to join the Brigade. With the Amphibious Warfare Squadron also based on Malta augmented by ships brought out of reserve, 3 Commando Brigade was ready for the

Reinforcements landing from landing craft at Port Said soon after the main assault, 1956

amphibious assault on Port Said, Operation *Musketeer*.

On 6th November 40 and 42 Commando, supported by 6th Royal Tank Regiment stormed the beaches of Port Said in LVTs and LCAs under cover of heavy Naval bombardment with the Fleet Air Arm strafing Egyptian positions. Once their first objectives had been taken against light opposition, 45 Commando were landed by naval helicopters from the training carriers *Ocean* and *Theseus* in the first ever helicopter assault. Heavy street fighting continued and by late that day the Commandos had seized the port and joined up with 3 Bn Parachute Regiment who had taken Gamil airfield the night before. What had been a highly successful military operation was brought to a sudden end by politicians in London calling a cease-fire at midnight. Ten Royal Marines had been killed in action. When troops were withdrawn and relieved by a United Nations force, 3 Commando Brigade returned to Malta and later 42, aboard HMS *Ocean* went back to UK where they arrived just before Christmas. The following year an enlarged Troop of over 100 men from the unit spent eight months in Londonderry on anti-IRA patrols.

Cyprus

For the next two years 40 and 45 Commandos, based in Malta, were continually engaged on a rotation basis in anti-terrorist operations in Cyprus against rebel General Grivas' EOKA guerrillas, much of it in the inhospitable Troodos mountains. It was at this time that, following on from the success of its helicopter assault at Port Said 45 Commando formed 'Heliforce' consisting of two rifle troops and a flight of four Fleet Air Arm Whirlwind helicopters. The Port Said operation had demonstrated the flexibility of carrier borne helicopter operations. The United States had already developed helicopter techniques in Korea and the French had made use of the concept in North Africa.

45 Commando searching a village in the Troodos Mountains, Cyprus 1958

Operation *Musketeer* had an uplifting effect on the future of the Corps and the amphibious assault concept of World War 2 came under scrutiny. The Defence White Paper of 1957 announced huge cuts in expenditure and manpower, the ending of National Service and a greater reliance on nuclear weapons for the defence of Europe. However it also saw the birth of the Commando Ship concept, particularly designed for operations outside Europe and, as far as the Corps was concerned, mainly in the Far East.

HMS *Bulwark* was designated the first Commando Ship and commissioned with 848 Naval Air Squadron at the end of 1959 and on 14th March 1960 42 Commando, brought up to strength, embarked for the Far East. The following year work began on converting HMS *Albion* as a second Commando ship; and in October that year 41

70

Commando was the first commando unit to reorganise from five 'fighting troops' to three rifle companies. One by one the other units followed suit over the next twelve months.

Royal Marines emplaning in helicopters aboard HMS *Bulwark*, the first Commando ship.

Aden

In 1960, 45 Commando moved to Aden in what was to be a tour lasting seven years of internal security operations in the Aden Protectorate and a bitter struggle during the long drawn out campaign in the mountains of the Radfan. There was a short operation in 1961 by both 45 Commando from Aden and 42 Commando from Singapore

71

45 Commando searching suspects in Maala whilst
carrying out internal security duties, Aden 1967

in support of Kuwait illustrating the remarkable flexibility and capability of this new amphibious concept. In 1964, when army mutinies in the newly independent East African nations broke out, 45 Commando embarked in the light fleet carrier HMS *Centaur*, and stood by off the coast ready to aid Zanzibar and Tanganyika. The Commando was airlifted ashore when called for and surprised the dissident military with the swiftness of their helicopter operations. On their return to Aden for operations in the Radfan, '45' were

45 Commando in the Radfan being resupplied by
Beaver and Twin Pioneer aircraft at Monks Field, 1963.

72

relieved by 41 Commando, which had been flown out to Kenya from the UK. When the final withdrawal from Aden was announced in 1967, 42 Commando embarked in *Albion*, arrived from Singapore, and 45 Commando was flown back to UK. The two Commandos were the last units to leave the beleaguered former colony on 29th November.

Confrontation in Borneo

Also in 1961 Headquarters 3rd Commando Brigade had left Malta for Singapore to be joined in 1962 by 40 Commando. It was not long before they were called on once again when the Brunei revolt erupted on 8th December 1962. 42 Commando were among the first to be flown across and L Company, under Captain Jeremy Moore, were immediately ordered to Limbang, 10 miles up river in Sarawak, where rebels had seized the British Resident, his wife and a dozen other hostages. Assisted by sailors from the minesweepers HMS *Fiskerton* and *Chawton*, they commandeered two Z craft and sailed up the river arriving off Limbang before dawn on 12th December. After being greeted by machine gun and rifle fire they ran into the beach and in a sharp engagement not only disposed of the rebels but also rescued all the hostages alive. Meanwhile *Albion*, which had been exercising with 40 Commando off the coast of East Africa raced across to deliver the unit into Sarawak by 14th December.

A Commando stick landing from a Wessex helicopter in Borneo 1966.

73

The Indonesian confrontation lasted nearly four years and for much of 1963 HQ 3 Commando Brigade, and its two commandos, supported initially by Royal Naval helicopter squadrons and later by the RAF, carried out rotating tours of duty in jungle fighting against insurgent Indonesian opposition. The Royal Marines Commandos, along with eight Gurkha battalions bore the brunt of the Borneo campaign and between December 1962 and September 1966 there was always at least one commando deployed there. Like all jungle operations, contacts were rare but an extremely high state of alertness was essential at all times. The Corps lost 16 killed and 20 wounded.

In 1964 the Corps celebrated its Tercentenary. Amongst a number of events held in July Her Majesty The Queen dined with the officers in the Painted Hall of the Royal Naval College Greenwich.

The parade for the Lord Mayor of London as part of the Tercentenary celebrations, 1964

Earlier in the day she reviewed a representative parade in the grounds of Buckingham Palace. It was at this parade that one contingent wore Lovat uniform for the first time. She said, *"For 300 years the Royal Marines have served their country with devotion and courage. I am confident that, as long as Britain needs to be defended and to play a part in preserving peace throughout the world, they will have an honoured place in the armed forces of the Realm."* Other celebratory events were held wherever Royal Marines were serving. On the last day of Tercentary Year, 27th October 1965, Admiral of the Fleet, the Earl Mountbatten of Burma, who for many years had been a staunch supporter of the Corps, was honoured in a unique manner by being

HRH The Duke of Edinburgh, Captain General RM with his uncle, the Earl Mountbatten of Burma after the latter's installation as a Colonel Commandant RM.

appointed the first Colonel Commandant for life.

Two decades had passed since the end of the war and the Royal Marines had not only found new roles in Commandos, landing craft and in the Special Boat Squadron but had acquitted itself with professionalism around the Globe in the many 'brush fire wars'. The old RN landing craft base at Poole became a Royal Marines establishment in 1956, when the Amphibious School moved there and was joined by the Technical Training Wing in 1973, both from Fort Cumberland at Eastney. Also in 1973, as part of the run down and eventual closure of Eastney Barracks, the Signals Training Wing moved to Lympstone, which had become the Commando Training Centre in 1970 and also absorbed recruit training from the Depot at Deal in 1976.

Chapter 8

The End of the Empire
1970-1981

By 1967 the end of the British Empire was dawning, former colonies and dependencies were being granted independence and there was no longer a need for a major British presence east of Suez. During the sixties both 41 and 43 Commandos had been reactivated for short spells, Portsmouth and Plymouth Groups had been reorganised as functional commands and the Corps strength stood at just over 8,000, of whom 800 were in the Band Service. RM Detachments had been removed from the few remaining capital ships, but they were retained in certain vessels such as the ice patrol ship, HMS *Endurance*, and the Royal Yacht, *Britannia*. For a period, small 22 man detachments were embarked in frigates with a subaltern as OCRM and a sergeant as the Sergeant Major, but even they were later reduced to only ten men under a SNCO, before being removed altogether by 1984.

The Royal Yacht Band aboard SS *Gothic* during the Royal Tour 1953/54

Since leaving Aden in 1967, 45 Commando settled into Stonehouse Barracks, Plymouth and took up their new role in the Strategic Reserve. 3 Commando Brigade withdrew from the Far East

76

in 1971 with a joint farewell parade in HMS *Simbang* on 18th March, when at sunset the White Ensign was hauled down for the last time. 42 Commando was the first unit to return settling into Bickleigh Barracks on 19th July. Headquarters 3 Commando Brigade followed taking up residence in Stonehouse Barracks, Plymouth, while 40 Commando, which had managed a short spell of duty in Hong Kong the previous year, arrived home just in time for Christmas 1971 and, returning from leave after the New Year, moved into Seaton Barracks, Plymouth. 45 Commando had moved up to Scotland in the spring of 1971 and took over the old RN Air Station at Arbroath. It was at this time that serious thought was given to establishing a Defence School of Music for all three services based on the Royal Marines School of Music at Deal. However after a lengthy examination the idea was dropped but the future of Eastney Barracks was also under discussion and eventually an announcement made that the unit there would close. In 1973 the Drafting, Pay and Records Office, Royal Marines (DPRORM) was absorbed into HMS *Centurion* at Gosport, and by 1991 the Corps Museum at Eastney was left, for the time being, as the only Royal Marines presence in Portsmouth.

Just prior to leaving the Far East, elements of 3 Commando Brigade aboard HMS *Bulwark, Intrepid* and the LSL *Sir Galahad* had raced to a major flood disaster in East Pakistan (now Bangladesh) and carried out important relief work. Meanwhile in the UK, 41 Commando as the 'Spearhead Battalion' had embarked on the Corps first emergency tour of duty in Ulster in September 1969 shortly after the troubles blew up there, to be followed by 45 Commando in 1970, fresh from their move to Scotland. Based in the Crumlin Road area of Belfast 45 Commando saw some of the worst of the violence, a grim portent of the many years to come *(see The Ulster Problem on page 82).*

Major Reorganisation

In England there had been other new developments and events. Both 29 Regiment Royal Artillery from 1961, and 59 Independent Squadron Royal Engineers from 1968 had provided field support for 3 Commando Brigade in the Far East and had by now been designated 'Commando' having become an integral part of the Brigade. For many years the Brigade had relied on the army for

77

their principal logistic support and in 1971 various logistic sub-units were brought together to form the Commando Logistic Regiment, which also included a Medical Squadron largely composed of RN personnel. The Regiment became a Royal Marines unit in 1974, and was initially commanded alternately by a Royal Marines officer and an Army officer (RAOC, RCT or REME). All ranks in these supporting elements had to earn their green beret before their postings were confirmed. In 1974, both 41 Commando, then based in Malta and 40 Commando, as the 'Spearhead Battalion', were deployed to Cyprus following the Turkish invasion of the island. Royal Marines detachments served in many of the frigates involved in the dispute with Iceland over fishing grounds in the mid-70s and known as the Cod War.

To celebrate the Silver Jubilee of HM The Queen in 1977, 42 Commando provided the main unit for the parade for Her Majesty on Plymouth Hoe on 5th August with other units providing displays. It was also that year that 41 Commando was due for disbandment but, having Trooped the Colour before Lord Mountbatten in Malta as their

In her Silver Jubilee year HM The Queen reviewed the Royal Marines on Plymouth Hoe

78

final parade, the unit returned to the UK only to be immediately reformed at Deal. The following year they represented the Royal Marines when they carried out London Duties for only the second time in the history of the Corps. In addition to providing guards on Buckingham Palace and St James's Palace, they also mounted guard at the Tower of London

The late 1970s also concluded a 10-year period when up to eight officers at any time were seconded to the Sultan of Oman's Armed Forces to help defeat the Yemeni-backed insurgency in Dhofar. Since the withdrawal of Britain's forces from most overseas bases, government policy led to a new and demanding role for the Royal Marines within NATO. For the early part of the 1970s the

Ski-jøring behind a BV202 during winter warfare training in Norway, 1979

Corps principal commitment was to NATO's Southern Flank, the Mediterranean area, but also in 1970 the first Royal Marines unit, 45 Commando, acquired a mountain and arctic warfare role in Norway to support the Alliance's Northern Flank. By 1979 the whole of 3 Commando Brigade was committed to arctic warfare. In addition, Commandos took their turn with Army units for four-month, and occasionally twelve-month tours in Northern Ireland *(see The Ulster Problem)*, and also in Belize; they carried out United Nations tours in Cyprus in 1979 and 1984, and the tactical headquarters and one company of 42 Commando was sent at short notice to the New Hebrides (now Vanuatu) for the independence celebrations when trouble was expected. The Corps was now tasked with maritime security within the UK and its exclusive economic zone, becoming the established experts at the protection of offshore oil and gas installations, whilst units, both large and small, were always available for other operations outside the NATO area when required. The changing role of the Royal Navy saw a decrease in the size of detachments at sea and the advent of the integral ship's helicopter in the late 1960s had given sea-going Marines a new challenge.

In the realms of amphibious warfare, the Royal Marines, together with the Royal Navy, had experienced the scrapping of the two LPHs (Landing Platform Helicopter) and the decision to scrap the two LPDs (Landing Platform Dock). By 1980 the strength of the Royal Marines was down to about 7,500 with the Royal Marines Reserve providing support with a further 1,000 men. The units of 3 Commando Brigade were stationed mainly in Devon, with 45 Commando at Arbroath, whilst the independent 41 Commando occupied Deal when it was not deployed operationally until it was disbanded in the following year. It was in May 1980 that Comacchio Company (named after the World War 2 battle in Italy fought by 43 Commando) was formed at Arbroath. This Company, later Comacchio Group and now the Fleet Protection Group, assumed responsibility for the security of certain Royal Naval establishments in the UK. It also continued to develop the 'Oilsafe' techniques pioneered by L Company of 42 Commando in 1977 to safeguard Britain's offshore gas and oil installations. The Royal Marines also provided the Special Boat Squadron, based at Poole in Dorset, which since the war had been the experts in beach reconnaissance, underwater swimming, and had a wealth of experience in anti-terrorist operations.

Continuing Operations

In the autumn of 1979, 42 Commando completed an emergency tour in Hong Kong to help the British Forces stationed there in their role of assisting the Royal Hong Kong Police (RHKP) deal with an unprecedented illegal immigration crisis.

Ranks from 3 Raiding Squadron searching a Hong Kong fishing vessel for illegal immigrants, 1979

During their time in the colony, they pioneered the use of raiding craft in sea borne Anti-Illegal Immigrant (II) patrols. Their success in apprehending large numbers of IIs attempting the sea crossing persuaded the Hong Kong Government to ask for a continuing RM presence, and thus it was that in April 1980, 3 Raiding Squadron (3 RSRM) was born. Initially equipped with Avon Searider Rigid Inflatable Boats (RIBs), the Squadron found itself being increasingly outrun by faster speedboats.

The introduction from September 1984 of the Fast Pursuit Craft (FPC) allowed the Squadron to regain superior capability and in the first 6 months after its introduction, 21 'Snakehead' speedboats were successfully intercepted. The Squadron comprised two Officers, a WO2, two SNCOs, 31 Cpls/Mnes and 12 RN locally enlisted able seamen. Following declining levels of II activity and the increased capability of the RHKP Small Boat Unit, it was decided that 3 RSRM should be disbanded on 1st July 1988. During its existence, the Squadron conducted some 1800 patrols, 26 Forward Operating Base operations, 4,200 boardings and had arrested 954 Illegal Immigrants, 36 other lawbreakers and apprehended 65 speedboats.

81

They also assisted with several rescues and other incidents, including two when they came under fire. After disbandment, a small RM presence remained in Hong Kong with a Lieutenant and a Colour Sergeant joining the Staff of the Senior Officer Hong Kong Squadron to co-ordinate three 3-man detachments operating FPCs from HM Ships *Peacock*, *Plover* and *Starling*. They remained there until the Colony was handed over to the Chinese in 1997, thus continuing a tradition of RM involvement in the territory that dated back to the possession of Hong Kong Island in 1841.

The Ulster Problem

Twentieth Century unrest in Ireland dates from its early decades when Royal Marines were twice sent to the south of the country; in 1916 to help quell the rebellion and again in 1922 when the 8th Battalion spent two years there. In 1957 elements of 42 Commando had spent eight months in Ulster on anti-IRA border patrols. It was in late September 1969 that 41 Commando, as 'Spearhead Battalion' and ready to move anywhere in the world at immediate notice, was sent to the Divis Street area of Belfast. The

following year, 1970, saw 45 Commando arriving in Belfast on 1st June for the first of many tours in the province.

Since then Royal Marines Commandos have regularly taken their turn with Army battalions and units in internal security operations in Ulster. From 1st March 1979 40 Commando spent a year in Londonderry, based at Ballykelly, and was not very far away from

Wearing flak jackets, the Band of Commando Forces entertains in Belfast City Centre, 1972

82

where Admiral of the Fleet the Earl Mountbatten of Burma (and a Colonel Commandant of the Royal Marines) was brutally assassinated by the IRA, whilst holidaying with his family at Mullaghmore on 27th August.

In the early days there was little modern day internal security equipment, such as batons and shields and the military had to face their tormentors unprotected. The Marines lived in rough quarters, their sleeping bags being crowded into large rooms, or even garden sheds. Sometimes these were factories, other times requisitioned schools. The Quartermaster and his staff, responsible for the supply of rations, clothing and ammunition, had only unarmoured vehicles in which to visit the outlying company locations. Protective clothing was slowly developed through the 1970s when flak jackets and special helmets with visors were introduced. Gloves and other specialist clothing, new weapons, anti-riot shields and CS grenades were brought into use. Later still night vision equipment was developed, giving the better surveillance capability at night. Armoured personnel carriers were used for transit whilst Land-Rovers and other light vehicles were protected with armour and wire mesh. The terrorists became more sophisticated in their methods and counter measures were devised against such weapons as improvised mortars and elecrically initiated mines that restricted movement, other than on foot, to helicopters in high risk areas. Patrolling was initially done on foot in four man groups. As there was no need for heavier weapons, the Marines of Support Company and Gunners from associated Royal Artillery batteries became foot soldiers. Each Commando would develop its own tactics and drills for dealing with its own particular area. On occasions Commandos were based in the built-up areas of Belfast and Londonderry, at other times on the border in South Armagh, where completely different tactics were evolved.

On 31st July 1972, 22,000 British troops were involved in Ulster in Operation *Motorman* that successfully cleared the 'no-go' areas of West Belfast and Londonderry. Royal Marines and Royal Naval personnel manned the four landing craft that took Royal Engineers bulldozers up the River Foyle into the heart of Londonderry. 40, 42 and 45 Commandos were involved. The saturation of the Catholic districts of both cities forced the terrorists to relinquish control, and allowed the security forces to move into a new phase of the campaign. Knowing they were up against a professional enemy, every man had to remain fully alert at all times, prepared for the unexpected, the sniper, the carefully laid bomb or the ambush.

The troubles did not only affect the Corps deployed to Northern Ireland for in 1981 an attempt was made on the life of the Commandant General Royal Marines, Lt Gen Sir Steuart Pringle, whose car was blown up by a terrorist bomb outside his London home and he suffered serious injuries. Much later, on 22nd September 1989, eleven Royal Marines musicians were murdered when a bomb was planted at the Royal Marines School of Music at Deal.

During this time, emphasis had been given to long-term intelligence and patrolling, winning the hearts and minds of these complex people,

41 Commando was one of the first units in Northern Ireland at the start of the emergency in 1969 and RM Commandos have continued to carry out regular tours in the province.

divided by their own religious beliefs. Patrolling the streets or countryside is a lonely and difficult task when the civilian population are trying to live as normal a life as possible. It is a frustrating and bitter struggle that the security forces are engaged in. It is often difficult for the Marine who comes from the mainland to understand the inbred hostility that exists between the various factions in Ulster. But this is just another job for which the regular serviceman must be trained, learning new skills to meet the special demands of fighting terrorism.

This memorial, to the eleven band ranks killed when an IRA bomb exploded at the RM School of Music in 1989, now stands in a Garden of Rest adjacent to the site of the old Concert Hall in Canada Road at Deal, which was later burnt down in 2003.

Royal Marines Commandos carried out more than 40 tours and they lost 14 killed and 95 wounded in those bleak years. Until a political solution is found there can be no real peace in the Province. In the meantime the security forces continue to act as they have always done, striving to maintain the rule of law and defeat terrorism with the Royal Marines continuing to play their part in the defence of freedom and the cause of peace.

The late 1970s had seen successive cutbacks in British defence forces, but in 1981 the Government Defence White Paper threatened to reduce the Royal Navy to little more than an anti-submarine force for the North Atlantic. The Corps existence was once again in jeopardy. When the Argentines invaded the Falkland Islands in the following year, it presented the Corps with an amphibious task for which they were highly suited.

Chapter 9

The Falklands War
1982

3° Commando Brigade were immediately despatched to the South Atlantic and played a major part in the recapture of the Falklands. Over fifty per cent of the total Royal Marines strength of 7,500 men were involved in the Falklands War. It was the perfect scenario for the sea-soldier, now turned commando, with an amphibious assault, a rugged approach march and a tough final battle in adverse conditions of both weather and terrain. Royal Marines were engaged in all phases of the campaign. They served as detachments in many HM Ships, as crews of landing craft, as commandos on the ground and as light helicopter pilots in the air. The Special Boat Squadron carried out highly important surveillance and reconnaissance. It was total involvement by the Corps.

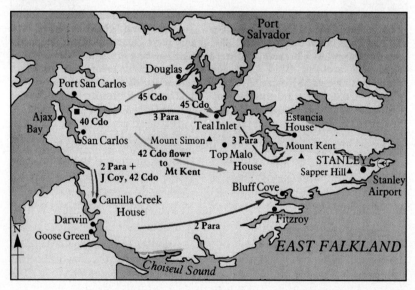

The Royal Marines had provided a small garrison in the Falkland Islands at various times in the 19th Century. HM Ships landed their detachments there regularly in the 1940s and 50s, but in 1965 Naval Party 8901 (NP 8901) was established. This was a permanent Royal Marines garrison and in 1982 numbered 37 all ranks. Men normally did a one-year tour but many volunteered for a second tour in this small dependency 200 miles off the Argentine coast. Others married local girls on leaving the Service and settled there. Such was the Royal Marines background to the invasion of the islands by the Argentines on the night of 1st/2nd April 1982.

It was mere coincidence that the force was double its normal size as the new NP 8901 had just arrived to take over from their predecessors. When first indications of an Argentine invasion were received, the Royal Marines prepared their defences, particularly in the airport area and around government buildings. With an area equivalent to that of Wales and a coastline three times as long, it was impossible to defend, or even observe, more than small stretches.

Argentine Special Forces landed in the early hours of 2nd April taking a cross-country route to make a devastating attack on the Marines base, which had been evacuated a few hours earlier. Soon after first light 1,000 assault troops with armoured personnel carriers swamped the town. There was some brief resistance from the Marines but, in view of the overwhelming odds, Governor Rex Hunt ordered the Royal Marines to surrender to avoid civilian casualties. Earlier in March HMS *Endurance* had landed her RM detachment to watch a party of Argentine scrap metal merchants on South Georgia, 800 miles east of the Falklands. The detachment based itself alongside the British Antarctic Survey Base at Grytviken. On 3 April the Argentines also attacked the island and after $2^{1}/_{2}$ hours fighting, in which an enemy helicopter was shot down and a corvette hit, the Marines were forced to give in against overwhelming opposition.

Within 24 hours of the Argentine invasion, the first British warships sailed south as a preliminary to the re-occupation of the islands. An Amphibious Task Force sailed within a week carrying the whole of 3 Commando Brigade, including its own Gunners and Sappers, plus 2nd & 3rd Battalions of the Parachute Regiment, combining to form the toughest fighting force in the world. Although many men had been on Easter leave and some were holidaying abroad, the whole force was ready to embark within 72 hours.

In addition to the fighting element, the Commando Logistic Regiment and RN Surgical Support Teams supported the initial infantry force, along with the Commando Forces RM Band who provided stretcher-bearers and personnel for other tasks afloat and were also a morale boosting bonus. Two Troops of the Blues and Royals with Scorpion and Scimitar light tanks, and T Battery of 12 Air Defence Regiment RA with their Rapier missiles, a battery of 4 Field Regiment RA and a troop of 9 Parachute Regiment RE made up the remainder of the landing force.

Over 3,500 miles from Britain and halfway to the Falklands, the main Amphibious Task Force stopped off at Ascension Island to train, shake down and cross-load. 40 and 42 Commandos, with 3 Para, were embarked in the SS *Canberra*, one of 49 civilian ships take up from trade (STUFT). This equalled the number of HM Ships eventually involved in the campaign. Other units were in amphibious ships and Royal Fleet Auxiliaries. Amongst the stores were about 75 over-snow vehicles but little other transport was taken.

M Company 42 Commando searching Grytviken,
South Georgia during the Falklands Campaign, 1982

M Company of 42 Commando, with SAS and SBS backing, had recaptured South Georgia by 25 April supported by HMS *Antrim* and *Plymouth*. After initial reconnaissance by Special Forces in

88

appalling weather, the main attacking force was landed a short distance from Grytviken, and under the cover of a naval bombardment, advanced upon the Argentines and forced them to surrender.

The Landing Force was commanded by the Commander 3 Commando Brigade, Brigadier Julian Thompson who, with Commodore Mike Clapp (Amphibious Task Group Commander) became responsible for the detailed planning of the assault. The Task Force Commander was Admiral Sir John Fieldhouse, working from his headquarters in Northwood, Middlesex, while Rear Admiral 'Sandy' Woodward commanded the Carrier Battle Task Group, operating in the South Atlantic. Later, when 5 Infantry Brigade were sent south, Major General Jeremy Moore, the Royal Marines most decorated serving officer, became the Land Forces Commander, Falklands Islands. Detailed planning of the options for landing took place whilst the Task Force was at Ascension Island. However members of the Special Boat Squadron and the Army's Special Air Service had been landed secretly from submarines and helicopters from small ships from 1st May. Their task was to glean intelligence and information about the Argentine Forces, their strength and dispositions, and report. Many spent more than three weeks living in the open in appalling weather, in close proximity to the enemy. The special SBS task was to reconnoitre beaches, reporting on gradients, hinterland, and suitability for landing an enlarged Brigade.

Operations at sea, which included the sinking of the Argentine cruiser *General Belgrano*, and the loss of the destroyer HMS *Sheffield*, continued in the cold waters of the South Atlantic. In the air, Fleet Air Arm Sea Harriers patrolled the skies above the Fleet while remarkable long range bombing raids were carried out on Stanley airfield by Vulcan bombers from the UK, involving six in-flight refuellings.

At dawn on 21st May, 3 Commando Brigade carried out a virtually unopposed landing in the San Carlos Settlement on the west coast of East Falkland. It took six days to whittle down the Argentine Air Force but the determined enemy continued to cause considerable concern and damage to the ships and ground forces from the mainland 200 miles away. 45 Commando landed at Ajax Bay, 40 Commando and 2 Para at San Carlos Settlement, and 3 Para at Port San Carlos. 42

Commando initially remained afloat as the Brigade reserve, landing later that day. During the landings two RM Gazelle helicopters were shot down with the loss of three crewmen.

After consolidating for five days, including setting up a Brigade Maintenance Area and Field Dressing Station at Ajax Bay, 3 Commando Brigade began to break out from the bridgehead on 26th/27th May. 2 Para moved south to attack Goose Green on 28th May. This was a bloody battle against considerable odds during which the Commanding Officer, Lt Col 'H' Jones, was killed and later awarded a posthumous VC.

Whilst this action was taking place, 45 Commando, 550 men, started their long 'yomp' across East Falkland, through Douglas settlement to Teal Inlet. Their 35 miles route lay across some of the most forbidding country in the world. Ankle deep bogs, valleys of knee twisting grass and rock runs of boulders were covered in 14 hours with few stops and without sleep. Men carried up to 50 kg on their backs, their own equipment weighted down with spare mortar ammunition. Meanwhile 3 Para took a more southerly cross-country course to Teal Inlet. 40 Commando, much to their disappointment, were left to provide the defence for San Carlos.

Between 30th May and 5th June, 45 Commando and 3 Para moved forward to positions in the area of Mount Kent and Mount

45 Commando approaching Sapper Hill through a minefield in single file

Estancia. Meanwhile 42 Commando had been flown forward by helicopters on the nights of 30th/31st May and 31st May/1st June to take up positions on Mount Kent. From here the Commando moved to Mount Challenger. From these positions all units carried out a vigorous patrolling programme to dominate 'no man's land', and fix the Argentine positions.

On 30th May 5 Infantry Brigade (2 Scots Guards, 1 Welsh Guards and 1/7 Gurkha Rifles) had arrived off San Carlos and Maj Gen Jeremy Moore, the Land Forces Commander, came ashore to the beachhead. It was during 5 Infantry Brigade's subsequent move forward by sea to advanced positions at Fitzroy that enemy aircraft attacked the LSL *Sir Galahad* in Bluff Cove causing casualties of 50 killed and 60 wounded, many of them from the Welsh Guards.

There was a sharp engagement near Top Malo House when 19 members of the Mountain & Arctic Warfare Cadre, operating in a reconnaissance role, attacked Argentine Forces, killing five and taking the remaining 12 captive, 7 of whom were wounded, an excellent example of good planning, intelligence and execution.

For the next ten days, continuous patrolling by the forward units built up a detailed intelligence picture of the enemy defences and dispositions. Royal Engineers and Royal Marines assault engineers recced and mapped enemy minefields, while gunners of 29 Commando Light Regiment and 4 Field Regiment pounded enemy defences around Stanley controlled by their own and Naval Gunfire Forward Observers. RAF and Fleet Air Arm helicopters brought up stocks of stores and ammunition. The enemy, consisting of the well trained 5th Marine Regiment and the conscripted 4th, 6th and 7th Infantry Regiments, held strong positions on the barren, craggy hilltops. They were badly led in most cases, but still proved tough opposition.

Plans for a final co-ordinated Brigade night attack were laid and tasks were given as follows: 3 Para – Mount Longdon (to the north); 45 Commando – Two Sisters (centre); 42 Commando – Mount Harriett (in the south); all units would exploit forward if possible. 2 Para and units of 5 Infantry Brigade were held in reserve. The assault was launched on the night of 11th/12th June; initially it was a silent approach, but later as the attackers neared their targets they brought

91

down a barrage of naval gunfire, artillery and mortars.

The assaults were made uphill over open ground covered with strafing machine gun fire. 42 Commando did a daring encircling movement to catch the enemy on Mount Harriett in the rear; 3 Para had a tougher time before taking Mount Longdon against the Argentine Marines when Sergeant Ian McKay was awarded a posthumous VC; and 45 Commando had the difficult task of a flanking attack and then thrusting along a narrow ridge to the twin peaks of Two Sisters. By dawn, all the objectives had been taken, but the troops were exhausted and exploitation forward had to be left to fresh units.

The Argentine defenders were beginning to lose the will to fight. However there was one hurdle left before the lights of Stanley could be seen. On the night of 13th/14th June, 2 Para took Wireless Ridge to the north supported by two light tanks of the Blues and Royals without much trouble, but the Scots Guards faced the tougher task of capturing Tumbledown Mountain in a bloody 11-hour battle.

By dawn defeated Argentines were seen wending their way back into Stanley and white flags were prominent. At 1105 on 14th

45 Commando entering Stanley at the end of the Falklands Campaign

June the British troops were ordered to fire only in self-defence and the weary, battle-worn 'veterans' marched into Stanley. General Moore finally took the Argentine unconditional surrender in Stanley at 9pm that evening. Nearly 13,000 prisoners were taken and repatriated to Argentina within the next few days, whilst the British Marines and Paras sailed slowly home in the luxury and comfort of modern ships. When SS *Canberra* sailed into Southampton Water on a sunny Sunday morning of 11th July it was to a euphoric homecoming. The sheer scale of the welcome took them by surprise.

The Falklands War was but a short campaign. To mount a force to re-occupy a group of islands 7,000 miles away in the South Atlantic, within range of the enemy air force, was a remarkable achievement, which showed versatility, determination, flexibility and a high degree of military professionalism. The calculated decision to send a British Task Force to protect sovereign rights and the freedom of the individual against unprovoked aggression was undoubtedly fully justified. The cost was 255 British lives and 750 Argentines lost. The Royal Marines had lost 26 killed and added another feat of arms to its already illustrious amphibious history.

As a result of the Falklands war the government eventually drastically changed its naval policy, particularly regarding its surface fleet, and the Royal Marines grew in strength from this, although there was no increase in numbers.

Another change of Direction

In August 1982, the first Royal Marines detachment was sent to Diego Garcia in the Indian Ocean for security duties, and where they doubled up their military role with appointments as civil police and customs officers. There were also commando exercises in Norway and Brunei. 40 Commando which had moved into its new home in Taunton in 1983, spent four months as part of the UN peace-keeping force in Cyprus the following spring, and in September 1985 started an 8 month tour in Belize.

It was in 1986 that the new SA80 rifle was introduced into the Corps and 42 Commando had the honour of being the first unit to carry out Public Duties in London armed with this weapon, mounting guards on Buckingham Palace, St James's Palace, the Tower of London

and on this occasion Windsor Castle also.

On the operational front Royal Marines served in frigates of the Armilla Patrol in the Persian Gulf. This was the codename for the operation to escort and protect British ships in and out of the Persian Gulf, and between 1986 and 1988 some 1,020 ships were given this safeguard. On 23rd January 1986 HM Royal Yacht *Britannia*, with the RM Band and a small detachment embarked, was involved in the dramatic evacuation of over 1,000 British nationals from Aden during heavy fighting between Marxist elements in the former British colony, now the People's Democratic Republic of Yemen.

42 Commando carrying out the Ceremony of the Keys at the Tower of London in 1986.

The unification of Europe and the breaking down of the iron curtain in 1990 radically changed Britain's defence policy yet again. No longer were large military forces required to face the Warsaw Pact countries, and an emphasis was put on smaller, highly mobile military units ready to face any commitment at a moment's notice. This was just the sort of role that the Royal Marines cherish, with their highly skilled training where the emphasis is on physical fitness, individual initiative, mobility and adaptability.

94

Chapter 10

The Gulf War and a New Century
1983-2002

When Saddam Hussein ordered his Iraqi troops to invade Kuwait in August 1990, the British government was among the first to respond. Unlike the Falklands, this was an operation in which the Army and Royal Air Force would have the prime roles, with the Royal Navy being tasked to patrol the Persian Gulf. Although the United States provided the majority of the forces, the United Kingdom played the second most important role in the multi-national United Nations force.

At first the British response was limited to Naval and Air Forces to deter the Iraqi Forces moving on from Kuwait to Saudi Arabia or other Gulf countries. Royal Marines Air Defence detachments joined the Royal Navy's Armilla Patrol ships within hours of being ordered to move; these were followed quickly by Protection Teams for the naval boarding parties as the United Nations authorised economic sanctions. All these teams, using rigid inflatable boats to enable boarding to take place while target vessels remained underway, and Lynx

A boarding party exercise

95

helicopters to rope down onto ships, spearheaded the embargo efforts, preventing Iraq from receiving proscribed goods from the outside world.

As the United Kingdom contribution to the coalition grew so the Royal Marines involvement increased with substantial presence in the Allied Headquarters; security teams for the Royal Fleet Auxiliary vessels; the Royal Marines Band of the Commander-in-Chief Fleet on board the Primary Casualty Receiving Ship, RFA *Argus*, as stretcher bearers and medical orderlies; landing craft to assist in Mine Counter Measures operations; medical teams in the land based Field Hospitals; and men in the Naval Commando Helicopter Squadrons based in Saudi Arabia. In all 10% of the Corps was involved in Operation *Granby*.

When the fighting war had finished, the focus of attention turned to the plight of the Kurdish refugees who were fleeing from the retribution being handed out by the Iraqi Army. British Forces soon became involved in providing humanitarian assistance and protection to the hundreds of thousands of Kurds who had fled to the mountains along the Turkish/Iraqi border. Operation *Haven*, spearheaded by 3 Commando Brigade Royal Marines had begun.

In a situation reminiscent of the Falklands crisis, the Brigade Commander was in Norway when 3 Commando Brigade was earmarked (in 1982 he had been in Denmark). He returned, was briefed and flew to Turkey with his recce group to be followed quickly by the advance parties from 45 Commando, 40 Commando, the Commando Logistic Regiment and from the 1st Amphibious Combat Group (1 ACG) of the Royal Netherlands Marine Corps. The latter were a welcome addition to the Brigade, cementing relationships that stretched back over 20 years and which were unique in NATO. Within days 45 Commando were spearheading the move into Iraq to create the safe havens for Kurdish refugees. The speed of the operation was no more vividly demonstrated than by the men of 45 Commando who were on post- Northern Ireland leave one week, Turkey the next and moving into Iraq the following! In all over 4,000 British troops from all three services were involved with the 2,500 Royal Marines providing the fighting element. Major General Robin Ross, (Commander Commando Forces) was nominated as Joint Force

A Royal Marine is subjected to close scrutiny by a Zakhu
resident in Northern Iraq during Operation Haven, 1991

Commander in Turkey with the Force made up of Hercules transports and Chinook helicopters from the RAF, Naval Sea King helicopters, 3 Commando Brigade (with its normal helicopters, artillery, engineer and logistic support), 1 ACG and a battalion of Dutch engineers, and a medical team from Australia.

With disease spreading fast amongst the refugees in the wintry conditions of northern Iraq, the provision of shelter, food, water and medical supplies were the first considerations. The next concern was to encourage the Kurdish refugees to return either to United Nations controlled camps or their own homes. A firm liaison was built up between the forces and the British Overseas Development Agency volunteers.

Royal Marines turned their hands to these unusual tasks with enthusiasm and compassion, an essential quality in any serviceman. With 40 Commando providing emergency relief in the mountain refugee camps and 45 Commando and 1 ACG providing security in the safe havens, gradually the Kurds were coaxed down from their mountain camps and persuaded that it was safe to return to their homes.

By 15th July 1991, all the forces had withdrawn and a brittle peace restored. The three months had been very hard but satisfying work. 40 Commando left a company behind as part of the multi-national 'Rainbow Battalion', deployed in Eastern Turkey as a deterrent to any Iraqi aggression towards the Kurdish people. They finally withdrew in September 1991.

These operations highlighted the remarkable skills of the Royal Marines in changing quickly from an aggressive fighting force to a compassionate peace keeping force. It showed yet again how swiftly the Corps can react in a time of crisis and how important are initiative, diplomacy and versatility. These are all part of the make-up of the modern Royal Marine.

Towards the Twenty First Century

1998 was the year of the Strategic Defence Review that was particularly significant for the Corps: while many arms of the Services saw yet more cuts, a clear commitment was given to maintaining a national brigade-sized landing force, with the necessary associated shipping. By the turn of the century this endorsement had borne fruit in the shape of a variety of new ships and systems, either planned or imminent. In this year too the Corps was involved in an operation which in retrospect seems to have demonstrated the type of deployment of the future.

40 Commando embarked in HMS *Ocean* in Plymouth Sound

98

40 Commando took part in Operation *Ladbrook* in the Congo Republic. Arriving in Brazzaville via Ascension Island, they were prepared to assist in the evacuation of British nationals from Kinshasa in the Democratic Republic of Congo. In the event, they were not used, but it demonstrated once again the Corps ability to move men quickly, with assets such as hovercraft, to wherever they were wanted. Before two years were out the Corps was to return again to this troubled continent.

The break up of the Former Republic of Yugoslavia was a key feature of European politics in the 1990s, and the Corps still continued to be involved there in the new Century. In 1995 Maj Gen David Pennefather was appointed Commander Rapid Reaction Force Operations Staff in Bosnia Herzegovina with 74 officers and men. Royal Marines were involved throughout this conflict, as Liaison Officers, as United Nations observers, and in Public Relations duties.

The Millennial Year underlined the part the Corps plays in the defence arena, with some 78% of the Corps on operations at one point, and with exercises or deployments in 30 different countries. The many and varied tasks carried out in this year typify the challenges which resulted from the changing world order in the 1990s. They are of a nature in many ways very different from previous years, and give a pointer to the future.

The Commando Brigade maintained its role as a very high readiness formation available as part of the national Joint Rapid Reaction Force, which was set up in 1999. The Headquarters itself, supported by its Signal Squadron, and a Royal Marines Band, deployed to Kosovo in command of the Multi-National Brigade (Centre), with the task of supporting the UN Mission in Kosovo in attempting to restore order following the withdrawal of the Yugoslav Army; violence was endemic with Albanians settling scores with Serbs, and with turf wars developing between rival Albanian gangs.

The Headquarters commanded some 18 units, including 45 Commando, the Commando Logistic Regiment, a British infantry battalion, Royal Artillery and Royal Engineer units, and Swedish, Finnish and Norwegian battalions. 45 Commando had just returned home from six weeks jungle training in Belize before deploying to Kosovo, where they took over a base in the town of Pristina. Here progress was made in developing a police force and a credible judicial system, all against a background of intimidation and abduction of officials, armed robbery, and vandalism. The backdrop of political uncertainty surrounding the demise of the infamous President Milosevic provided an interesting run-up to the Kosovo elections, which were held in a benign environment, in no small way due to the efforts of 45 Commando and the rest of the multi-national brigade.

42 Commando provided the Corps main contribution to the Joint Rapid Reaction Force from April onwards. In March an Amphibious Ready Group (ARG) consisting of HMS *Ocean, Fearless* and support shipping sailed to the Mediterranean with the Commando Group embarked. After training in Portugal and France with NATO allies, plans changed in May due to events in Sierra Leone.

Here, there was a serious threat to the Government by the Revolutionary United Front, one of many rebel movements that was supported by neighbouring countries which coveted Sierra Leone's rich mineral resources, in particular, the diamond fields. Some 400 UN Observers, including some Royal Marines, were surrounded and taken hostage.

A patrol of 40 Commando in Sierra Leone, 2000

The ARG was diverted to play a leading part in the Joint UK Force deployed to help stabilise the situation and support the UN Force there: the largest Naval Task Force since the Falklands War assembled offshore for Operation *Palliser*. Only seven days had elapsed between re-embarkation of the ARG in France, sailing via Gibraltar and Dakar (where stores and men were embarked, and training undertaken) and arrival on task in Sierra Leone, after being poised offshore, they relieved 1 Para. Intensive patrolling took place both on land, to keep the rebels away from the airhead at Lungi, and on the rivers using *Ocean*'s landing craft and hovercraft from 539Assault Squadron. In addition training support was provided to the Sierra Leone Army. Having returned to UK, the Commando Group joined the ARG again to conduct exercises in Gibraltar, Ukraine and Turkey. In October the call to arms came again, and they found themselves en route to Sierra Leone for the second time in six months. An eight day operation gave them time to demonstrate the considerable firepower available to the Commando, and so issue a timely warning to the dissident forces opposing the UN.

Commando Structural Changes
Since the end of the Cold War in 1989, changes in the global security situation and Government policy had meant that the operational situations in which the Corps might find itself had dramatically changed. With a range of new equipment coming into service that would increase the firepower and mobility of Royal Marines units, such as that provided by the .5 machine gun and the 'Viking All Terrain Vehicle', and with the advent of a new generation of amphibious shipping, there was a need to optimise the Brigade's ability to meet its tasks. A study was undertaken which resulted in a major reorganisation of the Commando unit structure. It had not markedly altered since the change to rifle companies from the original troop organisation in the early 1960s. 'Commando 21' was conceived as a result of lessons learnt from previous operations and recent operational analysis; Commando units were restructured in the period 2000-2003 to allow them to hit harder, faster and more accurately.
In 2000, having just spent 6 months supporting the Royal

101

Ulster Constabulary in Belfast from their home base in Taunton, 40 Commando reorganised into this new 'Commando 21' structure, followed in successive years by the other two Commandos. This organisation was needed to take advantage of modern weapon systems, enhanced firepower and greater mobility, and to cope with the increasing pace of contemporary operations.

Closer Links with the Royal Navy

Since 1998 there had no longer been RM detachments in ships in the Fleet. CINCFLEET suggested that the Royal Marines should provide a Fleet Standby Rifle Troop (FSRT) consisting of six 6-man teams with a 4-man HQ ready to support Fleet operations world wide. These teams, which were originally provided by the Commando Units in turn, rapidly proved their worth and were constantly in demand. Amongst their many deployments they were aboard HMS *Cumberland* off Albania for possible evacuation of British nationals, in HMS *Cornwall* off Sierra Leone to protect British interests, and with HMS *Glasgow* off East Timor, where unrest followed the independence ballot in the capital Dili. In 2000 the task was added to those undertaken by Comacchio Group, whose main role remained the security of the national nuclear deterrent, but by now included amongst its other tasks was the provision of water-borne detachments in Northern Ireland, where they played a key part in securing the inland waterways and coastal areas. It had also become charged with the protection of the Fleet Headquarters at Northwood. In recognition of its changing and increased responsibilities the unit was re-titled the Fleet Protection Group in 2001 and moved from Condor Barracks, Arbroath, which it had shared with 45 Commando Group, to purpose built accommodation at Faslane.

This change of title of Comacchio Group epitomised the closer relationship of the Corps with the Royal Navy, and indeed the changing role of the Navy, as underlined by the concept of Littoral Warfare, and the increasing inventory of specialist amphibious shipping. More staff appointments in the Corps became open to Naval officers, and vice versa, with, for example, a Royal Marines officer as Commander of a Naval shore establishment, and a Royal Navy officer as Director of Training at Lympstone. In 1999 the decision was made to realign Royal Marines Officers' rank with officers of the Royal Navy and other services to remove existing ambiguity in corresponding rank. All serving officers between Lieutenants of 3 years seniority and Lieutenant Colonels were moved one rank higher, thus ending years of confusion over exactly what ranks Royal Marines equated to in other services – confusion which most officers had happily enjoyed. Perhaps the culmination of our integration with the Navy came when HQRM in Portsmouth, the successor to the Department of the Commandant General in London, was integrated into the new Fleet Naval Headquarters.

Major Alterations to Corps Organisation
        With the strength of the Corps gradually becoming smaller the rank of the Commandant General had also reduced. When General Sir Peter Whiteley was appointed C-in-C Allied Forces NW Europe in 1977, his relief as CGRM was a Lieutenant General, Sir John Richards. Similarly, when Lieutenant General Sir Robert Ross retired in 1996, his relief was a Major General. The appointment of Commandant General Royal Marines was eventually changed on 2nd April 2002, when it became secondary to his prime operational role as the Commander of United Kingdom Amphibious Forces (COMUKAMPHIBFOR), and as such was ready to deploy on operations and exercises with his battle staff. At the same time Headquarters Royal Marines, which had only existed as such for nine years, closed and was subsumed into the Fleet Headquarters; responsibility for Regimental affairs, individual training and the Reserves was vested in his deputed representative at Fleet Headquarters, a Colonel, with the appointment title of Director Royal Marines. This reorganisation gave the Corps the exciting opportunity to play a major role in the Joint Rapid Reaction Force. At this time too, the re-naming of Royal Marines Poole as 1 Assault Group RM more properly reflected its responsibility for training, parenting and co-ordinating all landing craft assets *(see Appendix D)*.
        The Royal Marines Band Service has also moved with the times. Once more reduced numbers and less bands, coupled with an even higher standard of musical recruitment, has ensured they lead the world in the realms of military music, besides having a support operational role. Just over a quarter of the Band Service of 350 (including 70 under training) are currently women whose recruitment started in 1992. As musicians and buglers, and on operations, they play their part admirably, but recruitment of women into the regular

Corps is still unlikely in the near future.

Given the type of people the Corps attracts, and the ethos and attitude it imbues in its members, it comes as no surprise that many take the opportunity to test their courage and endurance in adventurous activities. Throughout the 20th century, Royal Marines took part in such outdoor pursuits as regularly winning the Devizes to Westminster Canoe Race, the Three Peaks Race, mountaineering in

Cpl Alan Chambers and Mne Charlie Paton trekking across the arctic plateau to reach the North Pole in 2000.

the Himalayas, the ascent of K2, Mount McKinley in Alaska and single handed transatlantic sailing. In 2000 a Corporal and a Marine completed the first ever unsupported journey, on foot, to the North Pole, overcoming frostbite, exhaustion and appalling weather in the process. In 2001 two Corporals attempted to row across the Pacific, but at the 5,000 mile point they were run down by a fishing boat – leading to strong words, apparently, with its skipper! 2003 saw a Royal Marine on the summit of Everest as a member of a joint RN/RM expedition. Such adventurous activities give opportunities to experience exposure to hardship and danger in peacetime, experience which is invaluable in our training for war.

Chapter 11

International Terrorism – Operations In Afghanistan and The War in Iraq
2002-2004

As the new century unfolded with the devastating event of the terrorist attacks on New York on 11th September 2001, the world suddenly found itself at war with terrorism. Among the first troops to be involved were the Royal Marines, fortuitously on a major amphibious exercise in the Persian Gulf area. 40 and 45 Commandos with elements of other Corps units were soon deployed in Afghanistan, in operations against an enemy that was implicated in planning international terrorism. In November 2001, the SBS were the first formed body to enter the capital Kabul, followed by 40 Commando who established a presence in the city. By patrolling with

Royal Marines of 45 Commando deploy from an RAF Chinook in the mountains of South East Afghanistan during operations in May 2002

the local police force they prepared the ground for the International Security Assistance Force. Later they were joined by 45 Commando, who deployed on offensive operations, often carrying up to 100lb loads, working at altitudes of 13,000 feet, in mountainous country near the border with Pakistan. After two initial contacts in which they were outwitted and out-gunned, the enemy proved to be very elusive. Amongst many finds of mortar, rocket, artillery ammunition, and arms, some 20 - 30 truckloads of munitions were found in a cave complex, and were destroyed in a controlled explosion of spectacular proportions, together with remaining terrorist installations and materiel.

The fact that recruits straight from Lympstone could deploy successfully directly into the mountains, into a challenging, hot, and very hostile environment, validated the Corps rigorous basic training regime. On departure they could look with satisfaction on their achievement in denying the enemy vital ground and ammunition, and in bringing stability to an area that had been traditionally rife with terrorism, crime and banditry. As important as the combat operations was the humanitarian work carried out simultaneously, and whenever time permitted.

Meanwhile, amongst many other operations, the SBS, work-ing often with the Americans, became engaged in the rescue of a CIA agent from an Afghan prison revolt in which 500 al-Qa'eda and Taliban, many still armed, were held. For three days the SBS in the Mazar-i-Sharif region, brought down heavy fire and aerial strikes to quell the revolt and help release the American captive.

In September 2002, 42 Commando finished a very successful six months tour in Armagh in support of the civil authorities. Developing political initiatives had by now reduced the offensive stance of the military presence in the province, and it became possible to build relations with the civil population in a way unimaginable in the 1970s era of violence. More mundane, but vital for the safety of the UK population, was the provision of emergency cover in the wake of industrial action taken by the Fire Service at the end of 2002. Some 650 Royal Marines were involved, including 150 Bandsmen and women, who played their part in exemplary fashion. Nevertheless the annual Mountbatten Festival of Music went ahead in 2003, albeit with very reduced numbers.

Kuwait and Iraq

Following the allied liberation of Kuwait from the forces of Iraq in 1991, Saddam Hussein was required by the United Nations to disarm, and to declare and destroy his chemical, biological, and nuclear programmes. Despite his prevarication, obstruction and concealment over some years, the UN inspectors made some headway in discovering what weapons or materials existed, but in 1998 he expelled them. Later, in 2002, he reluctantly re-admitted them following a unanimous Security Council Resolution, but was unable to explain what had happened to the materials identified by the inspectors in 1998 (which included elements for producing chemical and bacteriological weapons). As Iraq failed to comply with the will of the United Nations, and based on the authority provided by a series of UN resolutions since 1991, the UK joined a US -led coalition that was prepared to use force as a last resort to secure Iraqi compliance. The overriding political objective was to disarm Saddam of his weapons of mass destruction, and to support the Iraqi people in their desire for peace, freedom and good government. Despite Security Council lack of consensus, coalition forces commenced operations against the

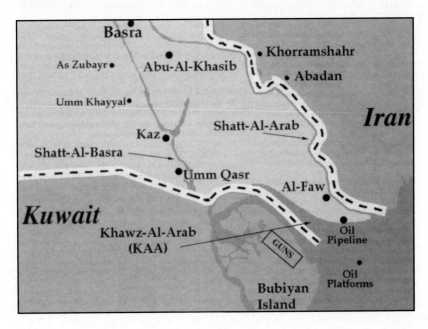

107

A Landing Craft Air Cushion of 539 Assault Squadron patrols the
Az Zubayr river near Umm Qasr.

regime on 20th March 2003, involving, eventually, some 46,000 service men and women, of which 3,000 were Royal Marines.

In January and February that year 3 Commando Brigade, (Brigadier Jim Dutton), deployed to the Middle East and commenced training; the attachment of the 15th Marine Expeditionary Unit USMC under command demonstrated the strength of our relationship with our American colleagues, and a squadron of their light tanks provided armoured support. At approximately 2000 hours on 20th March, 40 Commando led a helicopter assault to secure the area of an oil pipeline south of the town of Al Faw, with the objective of securing the oil facilities before they could be destroyed by the Iraqis. The first non-Special Forces to enter Iraq, they encountered light opposition from Iraqi irregulars, which they defeated, and despite being prepared for demolition, all objectives were secured without loss or destruction. The significance of this success should not be underestimated given the ecological disaster that would have resulted had demolition taken place.

In the early hours of 21st March 42 Commando landed, also

108

by helicopter, on the Al Faw peninsula. Deploying to the north-west of 40 Commando, they established a blocking position to prevent enemy interference with 40's objectives. The Brigade Reconnaissance Force landed alongside 40 Commando, but during their move a USMC CH-46 helicopter crashed in poor visibility, killing all on board – these included 5 Royal Marines, and 3 men from 29 Commando Regiment Royal Artillery.

After securing its initial objectives 40 Commando advanced towards Basra and over the next 72 hours came under repeated attack by Iraqi armour on their approach to the city. With the help of a Squadron of Challenger 2 tanks from the Queen's Dragoon Guards and surveillance and offensive support from the Naval Air Squadrons, the Commando destroyed a full Iraqi Armoured Battle Group. During this advance the Commando also had to fight a twenty-hour battle against an Iraqi Battalion whom they defeated, thus allowing the advance towards Basra. 42 Commando moved swiftly against opposition through Umm Qasr to allow them to lead the 'break-in' battle to this town. The Commando pushed through more serious opposition to achieve its objectives, culminating in the capture of Saddam Hussein's Basra Palace. After a brief period of consolidation within the city the Commando changed from a war role to a peace enforcement task within a matter of hours. They then proceeded to diffuse the local tensions and co-ordinate the distribution of much needed humanitarian aid. The Commando quickly reduced its confrontational posture and the young marine's ability to "win friends and influence people" came to the fore. Although the ensuing football matches with the locals did little to increase the Corps sporting prowess it did help greatly in reducing tension and engendering trust.

45 Commando supplied individual reinforcements to Brigade units, and company groups who operated either on separate tasks, or under command of the Brigade as appropriate, while those left at home were on stand-by as firefighters during a period of industrial action by the firemen.

539 Assault Squadron Royal Marines employed their full complement of craft to support all sea-based phases of the conflict. Hovercraft, landing craft and assault boats were all used to great effect during the initial amphibious assault and continued to have an

impact in clearing and securing the marshlands of southern Iraq. The Commando Logistic Regiment not only supported the Brigade throughout, but also used its supplies to support 1 (UK) Armoured Division, proving the invaluable nature of stocks held afloat on amphibious shipping. The Royal Marines Reserve, in their first compulsory mobilisation, deployed 117 ranks who served alongside regular Royal Marines displaying all the determination and commando spirit expected of them. The highest compliment that could be paid to these men was that they were indistinguishable from their regular brethren. The Royal Marines Band Service again also rose to the challenges put before them. The men and women provided continuous support in many forms, from medical and decontamination work, to morale boosting musical performances.

Meanwhile at Home

Elements of the Band Service were still returning from operations in Iraq and in support of the Fire Brigade dispute when the remaining members of the Band Service Beat Retreat on the lawns of Buckingham Palace for the Captain General's birthday in June 2003. The Band Service also marked the centenary of the establishment of the Royal Naval School of Music.

The main exercise at the beginning of 2004 was the Brigade (less 45 Commando) deployment of some 2,500 all ranks to Northern Norway at the beginning of 2004. The opportunity to train in this environment was highly beneficial as world events had so often overtaken our past planned winter deployments and have thus left a substantial skills gap. This was evident in the size of the novices' course at the start of January with some 1,126 Royal Marines having to qualify. By mid March the units were 'arctic capable' and moved on to their company and unit continuation training. The deployment culminated in a formation level exercise, Exercise *Joint Winter*, in which Brigade Headquarters was exercised through a high tempo scenario. The challenges that are faced in such a harsh and demanding environment create a standard of soldiering that can be adapted to any situation. The exercise also offered the opportunity to test the command capabilities of our new Landing Platform Helicopter HMS *Albion* with the Headquarters operating from her for the majority of

The new Landing Platform Helicopter, HMS *Albion*, during Exercise *Joint Winter*, 2004.

the exercise. The Headquarters also successfully transferred from ship to shore and tested their capabilities once on the ground.

In mid 2004 45 Commando came to the end of another successful tour in Northern Ireland, the fortieth such deployment by the Royal Marines. The Unit deployed to East Tyrone the previous December for a six-month roulement tour and had real success in supporting the Police Service of Northern Ireland in their own security operations. Interspersed with operational tasks, training in all aspects of amphibiosity continued. Exercise *Aurora* took place between May and July 2004 and was designed to improve working practices between the United States Marines, the Royal Marines and the Amphibious Task Group. The deployment involved elements of 42 Commando, Commando Logistic Regiment, Command Support Group and 539 Assault Squadron operating in the excellent training facilities of the USMC.

The RMR also continue to provide a very significant pool of manpower on Full Time Reserve Service (FTRS). 62 ranks were engaged with the regular Corps, the Naval Service and some tri-service establishments. This highlights the hard work and commitment that these Royal Marine Reserves, and their training staff, continuously undertake to maintain the highest standards of professionalism.

111

They are not just part time soldiers; they are men who want to deploy on operations and to serve the wider Corps.

The Future

The backbone of the Corps remains the Commando Training Centre at Lympstone. From the raw recruits taking their first steps towards earning the coveted Green Beret to the Advanced Command Courses that train our Sergeants Major, the Centre continues to produce the highest calibre of men required to meet the demands of the Royal Marines. Young officers follow a similar pattern of arduous training there. However, it is not just the training that CTCRM bestows on these young men, but also the esprit de corps, the ethos that all Royal Marines follow, and the unity that helps the Corps continue to operate as one of the world's elite fighting forces. The Royal Marines are a true expeditionary fighting force that can fight and survive in any environment around the world. This flexibility and thus employability on the world stage will continue to keep them at the forefront of modern warfare.

Royal Marines of all ranks are currently operating in 27 countries abroad. From a base of 6,000, they provide 40% of UK Special Forces. The SBS played a major, but as usual low profile, role in all recent operations: however their regimental identity changed in 2003, in order to fit more easily into the Special Forces sphere. Now able to recruit from all three services, greater unit cohesion was achieved by having a new common cap badge, rather than a mixture of badges from different arms. The new badge was a visible recognition of the achievement in passing one of the most arduous military selection courses in the world.

The uncertain climate in which we live guarantees that the future will hold multiple opportunities for the Corps, now steady at around 6,000 men, to play its part in Britain's defence strategy. The development of shipping and future weapon systems specific to the amphibious forces has placed the Corps in a favourable position, and by 2007 the Royal Marines will have an amphibious capability that has never been stronger. In an ever more uncertain world, whatever the future may hold, the Royal Marines will always be ready.

A Band of the Royal Marine Light Infantry c1895 *from a painting by Simkin.*

The Royal Marine Artillery c1897 *from a painting by Simkin*

45 Commando making the first helicopter assault, Port Said 1956 *from a painting by Lane*

The Assault on Limbang, L Company, 42 Commando, 1962 *from the painting by Cuneo*

"The Dhala Patrol", 45 Commando, 1965 *from the painting by David Shepherd*

"Commando Pick Up", Norway, 1979 *from a painting by Philip Marchington*

SS *Canberra*, "The Great White Whale" at San Carlos, 1982 *from a painting by Dean*

42 Commando's assault on Mount Harriett, 1982 *from a painting by Peter Archer*

The Massed Bands of the Royal Marines Beat Retreat on Horse Guards Parade,
London, on the occasion of the Captain General's birthday

With draped drums, the Portsmouth Band passes the Cenotaph in
London as part of the funeral procession of HM The Queen Mother, 2002

The Parade on Plymouth Hoe for the presentation of
New Colours to 40, 42 & 45 Commandos, 2001

An RM Lynx helicopter armed with TOW flying over Northern Iraq, 1991

A memorial service in Afghanistan 2002 to commemorate the
20th anniversary of the Falklands Campaign.

Appendix A

The Colours

The Queen's Colour

The Union Flag, in the centre of which is a foul anchor with the cypher of HM The Queen interlaced; above, St Edward's Crown surmounted by a scroll inscribed 'GIBRALTAR'; below, the globe surrounded by a laurel wreath, under which a scroll inscribed with the Corps motto 'PER MARE PER TERRAM'. The cords and tassels are of gold interwoven with silks of the Commando's colour which corresponds to the Commando lanyards worn by all ranks (see Appendix S).

The Regimental Colour

A Blue Flag with a small Union Flag in the canton nearest the pike head, and the Cypher of HM The Queen surmounted by a St Edward's Crown in the other three corners; centre embellishments are similar to the Queen's Colour, except that the foul anchor is interlaced with the cypher of George IV and the Commando numeral appears below the motto. The cords and tassels are of gold interwoven with silks of the Commando's colour which corresponds to the Commando lanyards worn by all ranks (see Appendix S).

Colours have been carried in the Corps since the first marine regiment was raised in 1664. At that time each company carried its own colour, which were all based on the yellow of the uniform. For succeeding regiments the company colours were altered with the times and to suit changes in the uniform.

By the time the Corps was reformed in 1755 as fifty independent companies, the number of colours in an army battalion had been to reduced to two. Colours do not appear to have been issued at first, probably because the independent companies were distributed between Chatham, Portsmouth and Plymouth and not organised as battalions. However in 1760, when a Battalion was formed for the expedition to Belle Isle, colours were provided. As in the army the King's or First Colour was based on the Union Flag and the Second Colour on a flag to match the regimental facings; the coloured material of the turned back skirts, lapels, collar and cuffs of the long coat worn at that time. Soon after this a stand of colours was presented to each of the three Divisions. The central devices were the same on both colours, namely a Foul Anchor within a wreath of roses and thistles.

It had long been the custom for 'Royal' regiments to have blue facings and so, after the Corps was so honoured in 1802 and when new colours were presented in 1811, the Second Colour, which by then was unofficially known as the Regimental Colour, was blue and so it has remained to the present day.

The first colours with devices similar to those borne today date back to 1827, when HRH The Duke of Clarence, later King William IV, the 'Sailor King', presented a stand to each Division. By this time in the army it had become customary to embroider on the colours battle honours which had been awarded to the regiment. In one of his speeches HRH spoke of this when commenting on the devices borne and said:

"The greatness of the number of actions to be considered and the difficulty of selecting amidst so many glorious deeds such a portion as could be inserted in this space, determined His Majesty King George IV to direct that The Globe encircled with Laurel should be the distinguishing badge as the most appropriate emblem of a Corps whose duties carry them to all parts of the Globe, in every quarter of which they had earned laurels by their value and good conduct....."

He pointed out that the honour GIBRALTAR was for the Capture and Defence in 1704-5 and he knew that *".......Marines were engaged in this capture and none but Marines were employed by the Prince of Hesse in the glorious defence.....".*

121

His Royal Highness went on to say that

*"........His Majesty has given them the most peculiar and honourable distinction, a badge of his own Cypher; and further, His Majesty directed that whatever King and Queen they might serve under hereafter, though the Cypher of the reigning Sovereign must appear on their Standard, still in those of the Royal Marines, the **Cypher GRIV** was forever to appear."*

He also said that the cypher "was being added to that peculiar badge **(The Anchor)**, which is your distinctive bearing" and drew attention to *"......the motto, peculiarly your own, 'PER MARE PER TERRAM' has been allowed to remain....."* He pointed out that in 1858 new Colours were presented to each of the four Divisions by the local Naval Cs-in-C with very little ceremony. The design followed a new pattern for Colours in the Army and departed from the embellishments authorised by King George IV. This change was most unpopular in the Corps and it is not surprising that when new stands were to be presented in 1894 and 1896, the 1827 design returned. However that was not the only change that was made. Until the middle of the nineteenth century Colours were nearly six foot square, on a 9ft 10in pike and were carried by very young officers, often mere boys in their late teens. These young men had considerable difficulty in controlling the Colours when they were unfurled, when even a slight breeze could carry them off their feet and they sometimes suffered the indignity of being thrown to the ground. The 1894 and 1896 stands were the first of a new smaller pattern to be carried in the Corps, 3ft 9in by 3ft, and the same size as those borne today.

In 1947, on the reorganisation into RM Groups, the Colours of Chatham, Portsmouth and Plymouth Divisions automatically became the Colours of RM Barracks, Chatham, Eastney and Plymouth respectively. The last of these to be carried were those of RM Barracks, Eastney, presented in 1956 and which were finally laid up in the Corps Museum in 1973. Since then only the Commandos have carried Colours in the Royal Marines.

Colours were first presented to Commandos in 1952, when HRH The Duke of Edinburgh presented a stand to each of the three units of 3 Commando Brigade RM in Malta. The Colours presented to 40 Commando RM at that time were laid up in the Corps Museum when new Colours were presented in 1976. Those of 42 Commando RM are now in the Officers' Mess at the Commando Training Centre RM, Lympstone, the unit having received a new stand in Singapore in 1968. In the following year HM The

122

Queen presented new Colours to 45 Commando RM in Plymouth, and their original stand was laid up in Stationers Hall in the City of London.

41 and 43 Commandos were reformed in 1960 and 1961 respectively and also received Colours. When 41 Commando disbanded their Colours were laid up in the Officers' Mess at Stonehouse Barracks, Plymouth but are now in the RM Museum at Eastney, whilst 43 Commando's Colours are in the Officers Mess of the Fleet Protection Group Royal Marines.

New stands of Colours were presented to 40, 42 and 45 Commandos by the Captain General at a parade held on Plymouth Hoe on 12th July 2001. The previous Colours of 40 Commando RM are laid up in St Lawrence Jewry next Guildhall in the City of London, the Corps Affiliated Church (*see Appendix I*), those of 42 Commando are in the Falklands Hall at the Commando Training Centre RM, and 45 Commando's previous Colours are in the Officers' Mess at Stonehouse Barracks.

In the Royal Marines there have only been two occasions when the Sovereign has presented Colours. Queen Victoria presented Colours to Portsmouth Division RMLI at Osborne House on the Isle of Wight in 1894. Her Majesty Queen Elizabeth II presented Colours to 45 Commando RM in Plymouth in 1969, but all the remainder since 1951 have been presented by HRH The Prince Philip, Duke of Edinburgh, including the last Colours to be borne by RM Barracks, Plymouth and RM Barracks, Eastney. The presentations to RM Barracks, Plymouth and the three units of 3 Commando Brigade in Malta were even prior to the appointment of HRH as Captain General Royal Marines.

The Corps Colours

The significance, proportion and sequence when worn horizontally is as follows:

YELLOW (Old Gold) – The coat colour in 1664 – one part
GREEN (Light Infantry Green) – Perpetuates Light Infantry title – one part
RED (Drummer Red) – The infantry tunic colour until 1876 – two parts
BLUE (Navy Blue) – The connection with the Royal Navy – eight parts

Corps Memorable Dates

23rd April – The Raid on Zeebrugge in 1918. Towards the end of WWI, the 4th Royal Marine Battalion landed on the Mole to enable the blocking of the entrance to the canal, which was being used by the Germans as a base for their submarines. Two Victoria Crosses were awarded to the battalion and no other battalion has since been numbered '4th'.

28th April – Gallipoli in 1915. The Royal Marine Brigade landed on the peninsula as part of the expedition to drive up towards Constantinople during the First World War. Together with 1 RN Brigade they bore the brunt of the Turkish attacks and displayed great resolution in this major amphibious operation.

6th June – The Landings in Normandy in 1944. During the Second World War, over 17,500 Royal Marines took part in the largest amphibious operation in history. They crewed most of the minor landing craft, manned the guns in the supporting capital ships and provided an Armoured Support Group, beach clearance and control parties and engineers. Five Royal Marine Commandos landed during the assault phase.

7th June – The Battle of Belleisle in 1761. On this island off the coast of France, two battalions of Marines served with great distinction at this siege during the Seven Years War. The laurel wreath in the Corps insignia is believed to have been awarded in honour of this distinguished service.

14th June – The Recapture of the Falkland Islands in 1982. The Royal Marines were involved in virtually every significant aspect of this successful campaign. The main landing was planned and executed by 3 Commando Brigade, with RM detachments in many ships of the Task Force and with all landing craft manned by Royal Marines.

17th June – The Battle of Bunker Hill in 1775. During the American War of Independence, after two unsuccessful assaults up the steep hill, which failed to dislodge the rebels, the 1st Marines and the 47th Regiment were committed to the battle. They took the position, after which it was reported that the Marines' "unshaken steadiness was conspicuous".

24th July – The Capture of Gibraltar in 1704, in the War of the Spanish Succession, was carried out by a brigade of British and Dutch Marines, who after the surrender successfully held the fortress against repeated attacks. Granted for the capture and defence of the Rock, this is the only battle honour borne on the Colours.

21st October – The Battle of Trafalgar in 1805 was the most decisive sea fight in British history and in which over 3,500 Royal Marines took part. In their traditional stations on the upper decks, they bore a brave and important part in Lord Nelson's success.

28th October – The Birth of the Corps in 1664 was when King Charles II sanctioned the formation of the first regiment formed specifically for service at sea. The yellow uniform of the Duke of York and Albany's Maritime Regiment of Foot is commemorated by the yellow stripe in the Corps colours.

1st November – The Assault on Walcheren in 1944, in which Royal Marines Commandos and Support Craft guns' crews successfully played a gallant and leading part, resulted   in clearing the entrance to the River Scheldt, thereby re-opening the Port of Antwerp to Allied shipping after the invasion of the Continent during World War II.

Unit Memorable Dates

HQ 3 Commando Brigade RM

21st May – The Landings at San Carlos Water, 1982. 3 Commando Brigade was the landing element of the amphibious task force ordered to recapture the Falkland Islands. Sound planning during the voyage south culminated in a successful Brigade night landing in the San Carlos region. The choice of this remote sheltered landing area enabled the landing force to withstand the constant air attack of the Argentine Air Force, and played a major part in ensuring the successful recapture of the islands.

The UK Landing Force Command Support Group

20th March – Operations on the Al Faw Peninsula, 2003. During 3 Commando Brigade operations to capture the Al Faw Peninsula in Iraq, the United Kingdom Landing Force Command Support Group operations commenced some 2 weeks before the Brigade landings. It was tasked with achieving information dominance over the enemy through surveillance, reconnaissance, electronic warfare, the provision of communications and the protection of Headquarters. The bravery and ingenuity of its members helped ensure that the Brigade maintained dominance over the forces arrayed against it. It had a pivotal role in the success of the Al Faw landings and the subsequent break-out to Basra.

40 Commando RM

3rd October – The Landing at Termoli in 1943. 40 Commando was part of a small force which landed at the seaport town under cover of darkness on the Adriatic Coast of Italy and behind the German lines. Complete surprise was achieved and by 0800 hrs the town had been captured.

20th March – The Clearance of the Al Faw Peninsula, 2003. During the liberation of Iraq 40 Commando RM mounted an amphibious helicopter assault and seized key oil infrastructure on the Al Faw peninsula. As the first conventional troops to cross into Iraq, the strategic significance of the operation was immense. In a two-week period of intense operations, they cleared a large expanse of enemy held terrain, and defeated a major enemy stronghold on the periphery of Basra. Their role in the success of the coalition operation was crucial and profound.

42 Commando RM

31st January – The Battle of Kangaw in 1945. In Burma, after two days of hand-to-hand fighting 42 Commando captured Hill 70. The unit was immediately subjected to heavy artillery fire and then, after a lull of several days and in spite of heavy casualties, beat off repeated Japanese counter attacks to successfully hold the position.

11th/12th June – The Attack on Mount Harriet in 1982 during the Falklands War was part of 3 Commando Brigade's main assault on the Argentine positions on the high ground overlooking Stanley. By moonlight and in freezing temperatures, the unit moved undetected through minefields to successfully surprise the enemy in their rear.

45 Commando RM

23rd January – The Attack on Montforterbeek in 1945. After hard fighting in bitterly cold weather during the campaign in North West Europe, the leading troops of the unit captured German positions holding up the advance through Holland. In spite of determined counter-attack and fierce hand- to-hand fighting the positions were held. It was for his bravery during this action that L/Cpl H E Harden RAMC was posthumously awarded the Victoria Cross.

11th/12th June – The Attack on Two Sisters in 1982 during the Falklands War was part of 3 Commando Brigade's main assault on the Argentine positions on the high ground overlooking Stanley. Bold reconnaissance by junior leaders had pin-pointed well equipped and dug-in Argentine positions. A silent night approach was made up the jagged, craggy rock formations, which after fierce hand-to-hand fighting culminated in the capture of the feature.

Commando Logistic Regiment RM

22nd May – The Landing at Ajax Bay in 1982. The support provided for the three weeks of the campaign from this area where they had landed, in adverse weather conditions and often under heavy air attack, was a battle winning factor of the Falklands War. This was entirely due to the skill, dedication and exceptional devotion of the various elements of the unit.

Operational Landing Craft Squadrons

6th June – The Landings in Normandy in 1944. In the assault on the German held French coast, Royal Marines manned the minor landing craft carrying the first and subsequent waves. For weeks after the initial assault they continued to ferry ashore men, vehicles and stores. Both afloat in landing craft and ashore in Naval Beach Parties, Royal Marines played a prominent and vital part in the invasion.

21st May – The Landings at San Carlos Water in 1982. At the start of the campaign in the Falklands, landing craft squadrons landed 3 Commando Brigade on to five separate beaches without loss. They continued to offload the logistics in deteriorating weather and under constant air attack. They later assisted in mine-sweeping duties, raiding and insertion tasks. The Task Force could not have achieved its objective without this invaluable contribution.

Fleet Protection Group RM

2nd April – The Battle of Comacchio in 1945. In Italy 43 Commando, to whom the Fleet Protection Group owes its origin, successfully achieved its objectives during a Brigade attack against strong opposition, in which it crossed a river in inflatable dinghies under fire. Next day, whilst moving across open country, the unit met intense fire and the leading troop was pinned down in the open. For his gallantry in drawing the enemy's fire, thereby enabling his Troop to move to cover, Cpl Tom Hunter was awarded a posthumous Victoria Cross.

Senior Royal Marines Appointments

The Captain General

HRH The Prince Alfred, Duke of Edinburgh was appointed Honorary Colonel of the Royal Marines in 1882. After his death HRH The Duke of Cornwall and York, later Prince of Wales, was appointed Colonel-in-Chief in 1901 and continued to hold the appointment when he ascended the throne as King George V. King George VI assumed the title when he came to the throne in 1936 and in 1948 changed the title to Captain General. On the occasion of her coronation in 1953, Her Majesty The Queen appointed HRH The Prince Philip, Duke of Edinburgh, Captain General of the Royal Marines. He wears the uniform of a Royal Marines General Officer with the badges of rank of a Field Marshal, crossed batons on a wreath of laurel with a crown above.

Honorary Colonel

His Majesty King Harald of Norway was appointed an Honorary Colonel in the Royal Marines by Her Majesty The Queen in 1981, when he was the Crown Prince. He wears the uniform and badges of rank of a Royal Marines Colonel.

The Commandant General

The Royal Marines General holding the appointment of Commander United Kingdom Amphibious Force (COMUKAMPHIBFOR) is also the Commandant General Royal Marines and wears the Royal Marines uniform and badges of his rank.

Colonels Commandant

These are honorary appointments which are held for four years normally by retired Royal Marines General Officer, but senior officers of other services may also be appointed. RM officers may wear either the uniform and badges of their rank on retirement or, as in the case of officers from other services, a RM General Officer's uniform with the badges of rank of a Colonel.

Honorary Colonels Royal Marines Reserve

Each Royal Marines Reserve unit may have an Honorary Colonel, who wears the regimental uniform of a Royal Marines Officer with the badges of rank of a Colonel.

Royal Marines Organisation – 2004

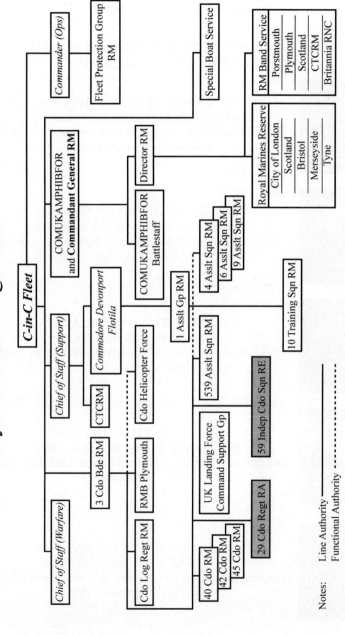

Notes: Line Authority ———
Functional Authority ------

Abbreviations have been used whenever meaning is clear.
Naval Staff are in italic.

The Victoria Cross

The following Royal Marines have been awarded
the highest British honour for gallantry:

CORPORAL J PRETTYJOHNS RM
The Battle of Inkerman 5th November 1854.
Successfully led a section which dislodged Russian
marksmen from some caves.

BOMBARDIER T WILKINSON RMA
The Siege of Sevastopol 7th June 1855.
Repaired damage to the advanced battery's revetments
under heavy fire.

LIEUTENANT G D DOWELL RMA
The Baltic 13th July 1855.
Rescued the crew of a rocket boat under intense 'grape
and musketry' fire.

CAPTAIN L S T HALLIDAY RMLI
The Siege of Peking 24th June 1900.
Led the way into some burning Legation buildings under
heavy small arms fire.

LANCE CORPORAL W R PARKER RMLI
Gallipoli 30th April 1915.
Displayed conspicuous bravery in rescuing wounded in
daylight under heavy fire.

All the VCs awarded to Royal Marines are on display in the Royal Marines Museum at Eastney, Southsea.

MAJOR F J W HARVEY RMLI *(Posthumous)*
The Battle of Jutland 31st May 1916.
Ordered the flooding of his turret's magazines although mortally wounded, thereby saving his ship.

MAJOR F W LUMSDEN DSO RMA
France 3rd April 1917.
Led a party to recover six enemy guns under heavy fire.

CAPTAIN E BAMFORD DSO RMLI
The Raid on Zeebrugge 23rd April 1918.
Led his company with initiative and daring in the face of great difficulties *(by ballot)*.

SERGEANT N A FINCH RMA
The Raid on Zeebrugge 23rd April 1918.
Maintained continuous covering fire from the exposed foretop, although severely wounded. *(by ballot)*

CORPORAL T P HUNTER RM *(Posthumous)*
The Battle of Comacchio 3 April 1945.
Advanced alone over open ground to save his Troop by offering himself as a target.

Honours and Awards

	1854 -1914*	World War I	1919-1939	World War II	1946-1993	1993 – 2003
Victoria Cross	4	5		1		
GCB					1	
GCSI			1			
GCIE			1			
GCMG			2			
GCVO			1			
GBE		1				
KCB	7	3	7	2	15	1
KCMG		1			2	
KCVO				1	4	
KBE				2	1	
CB	16	25	18	10	41	5
CMG	1	34		1	2	2
CIE				1		
CVO			1		3	1
CBE		17	6	20	31	8
DSO	8	64(5)		33(4)	6(1)	1
OBE		67	15	44	123	43
MVO	8		9		12	1
MBE		11	13	84	130	123
Conspicuous Gallantry Cross						4
Distinguished Service Cross		36(1)		50(2)	5	
Military Cross		57(2)		55(1)	33(2)	7
Distinguished Flying Cross					2	
Air Force Cross		2			2	1
Albert Medal		2	3			
Distinguished Conduct Medal	16 (2)	36		8	6	
Conspicuous Gallantry Medal	22	15		7		
George Medal				11	1	1
Distinguished Service Medal		192	1	194(1)	8	
Military Medal		317(12)		105(1)	52(1)	
Distinguished Flying Medal					1	
Queen's Gallantry Medal					24	12
Royal Victorian Medal (silver/bronze)	5		29		14	1
British Empire Medal		3	7	99	324(1)	3

*1854-1914 Gallantry Awards only
Bars to Awards shown in brackets

The Wilkinson Sword of Peace

Annually since 1967 a unit in each of the Services, which has done most to preserve friendship and peace in the territories in which it has served, is presented with an award by Wilkinson Sword Ltd. This award is a sword of the standard pattern used by the unit to which it is awarded, so that it can be carried on parade on special occasions and is normally referred to as a 'Wilkinson Sword of Peace'.

The original Sword of Peace was awarded by the Honourable East India Company in 1802 to First Lieutenant Samuel Snook of the Bombay Marine, a forerunner of the Royal Indian Navy, for exemplary kindness towards a party of refugees from the Pelew Islands in the Philippines which was stranded in Bombay without friends or means of support.

40 Commando was one of the first three units of the Services to receive the award in 1967 for its effort in winning the hearts and minds of the people of Sarawak in 1966. Since then the unit has been awarded the Royal Navy's sword on two further occasions; in 1973 for fostering good relations with he people of Belfast whilst in the province the previous year; and again after a tour of duty in Cyprus in 1984, when they were instrumental in re-uniting goodwill with the local community.

For their work with the people of the island, the 1977 sword was presented to Naval Party 8901 for their work with the scattered settlements of the Falklands Islands. Units of 3 Commando Brigade who took part in peace support operations in Kosovo were presented with the 2002 Sword.

The three Wilkinson Swords of Peace awarded to 40 Commando in 1967, 1972 and 1984

The King's Squad

On the occasion of his visit to the 4th Battalion in March 1918, preparing at Deal for their raid on Zeebrugge on St George's Day 1918, HM King George V also visited the Depot and witnessed recruit training. He was much impressed with what he saw and on completion directed that the senior squad of recruits under training should be designated 'The King's Squad'. As a mark of distinction it is customary for members of the squad to wear a white lanyard on the left shoulder of their blue uniform and to wear the chinstrap of their cap 'down' below the chin. At one time one of the highlights of the Royal Tournament was a drill display by the King's Squad of the Royal Marines. This was regularly performed up until 1959, but since then these displays have only been performed in 1980 and 1990. Today the senior recruit troop at the Commando Training Centre RM, Lympstone is titled 'The King's Squad'.

The King's Badge

Soon after his visit to Deal, HM The King further directed that the best recruit in the King's Squad should be awarded 'The King's Badge', *"provided he reaches the required standard"*. The senior recruit receives his

badge from the Inspecting Officer at the Squad's passing out parade. The gold wire embroidered badge, which consists of the Cypher of King George V (GvR) within a laurel wreath, is worn at the top of the left sleeve. It is worn throughout his service, in all orders of dress no matter what rank he later attains.

The Prince's Badge

In 1978, to commemorate his 25th anniversary as Captain General, HRH The Prince Philip, Duke of Edinburgh directed that the best all-round musician or

bugler completing training each year should be awarded the Prince's Badge. The silver wire embroidered badge, which consists of the cypher of HRH Prince Philip surmounted by a coronet all within a lyre, is worn on the top of the left sleeve. It is worn throughout his service, in all orders of dress no matter what rank he later attains.

Freedoms & Privileges

The Royal Marines enjoy a number of privileges which were earned by their loyalty, devotion to duty and good character, they include:

Freedom of Cities and Towns: The freedom of a city or borough is the most honourable distinction a local government council can bestow. Regiments granted the Freedom of Cities and Towns invariably march through the area with their "drums beating, bayonets fixed and colours flying" as a salute and a mark of respect to the citizens. The Royal Marines have been granted the freedom of:

Deal	1945	Exeter	1977
Chatham	1949	Medway	1979
Plymouth	1955	Newcastle upon Tyne	1989
Portsmouth	1959	Gibraltar	1996
Poole	1973	The Wirral	1998
Stanley, Falkland Islands	1976		

Affiliation: In addition the Royal Marines have been affiliated to the town of Exmouth since 1968.

Freedoms to RM Units: In 2003 the following granted the freedom to their local RM Units:

The County of Angus – 45 Commando RM
The Borough of Taunton Deane – 40 Commando RM
The Town of Dartmouth – RM Band of Britannia Royal Naval College

The City of London has the legal right to prevent troops freely entering the City. Since 1664 the Admiral's Regiment, and subsequently the Royal Marines, have been granted the privilege of marching through the City with drums beating, bayonets fixed and colours flying. The origin of this privilege lies in recruits for the Duke of York and Albany's Maritime Regiment of Foot being found from the Trained Bands of London. The privilege is shared with only six other regiments, The Blues and Royals, Grenadier Guards, Coldstream Guards, The Princess of Wales's Royal Regiment, The Royal Regiment of Fusiliers and The Honourable Artillery Company. (No regiment has the Freedom of the City of London) On 23rd April 1974 the Royal Marines were affiliated to the Church of the Corporation of the City of London, St Lawrence Jewry.

Royal Marines Prayers

The Royal Marines Prayer

O Eternal Lord God, who through many generations has united and inspired the members of our Corps, grant Thy blessing, we beseech Thee, on Royal Marines serving all round the GLOBE. Bestow Thy CROWN of Righteousness upon all our efforts and endeavours and may our LAURELS be those of gallantry and honour, loyalty and courage. We ask these things in the Name of Him, whose courage never failed, our Redeemer, Jesus Christ. **Amen**

The Royal Marines Band Service Prayer

Almighty and eternal Lord God, in whose sight and love live our memories of many generations of those who have served You in the Band Service of the Royal Marines: we thank You for the rich heritage of music placed in our hands, and for the joy and inspiration which it brings to men; enable us with our whole hearts to serve You, that by Your grace and through our gift of music, we may continue to inspire, help and lead men; we ask these things in the name of Jesus Christ our Lord. **Amen**

At Royal Marines church and drum-head services the following special second verse of *"Eternal Father strong to save"* is often sung:
O, Holy Spirit grant, we pray
To Royal Marines, both night and day,
The courage, honour, strength and skill
Their land to serve, Thy law fulfil
From every peril to our Corps.

Left Under the watchful eye of a Marine armed with a GPMG, the Chaplain of 45 Commando, using a makeshift altar, conducts a service during operations in the Radfan, 1963.

Associations with the City of London Livery Companies

The Worshipful Company of Stationers and Newspaper Makers adopted the Corps in March 1949. The Stationers' Trophy is awarded to the best trainee clerk or stores accountant who qualifies each year and the Cox Cup to the best student on IT/IS training courses each year at the Signals and Clerks Training Wing at the Commando Training Centre, Lympstone. The first Colours to be presented to 45 Commando RM are laid up in Stationers' Hall.

The Honourable Company of Master Mariners adopted the City of London Royal Marine Forces Volunteer Reserve (now RMR) in 1953. His Royal Highness The Prince Philip, Duke of Edinburgh, Captain General Royal Marines, is a Warden of the Court of the Master Mariners. Since 1964 the Commandant General has been an Honorary Member of the Company during his appointment.

The Worshipful Company of Musicians present a silver medal annually, which is awarded to the best student in the Bandmasters' Class at the RM School of Music. Another silver medal and a bronze medal, known as the Cassel Prizes, are awarded to the winner and runner-up in an annual competition for musicians under training at the RM School of Music.

The Worshipful Company of Armourers and Brasiers make an award to the best trainee armourer who qualifies each year.

The Worshipful Company of Plaisterers make an award to the best Signals NCO on the S1's Course each year. In 1983 the Company present-ed to the Corps a painting of SS *Canberra* during the landings at San Carlos which is now in the Officers' Mess at CTCRM, Lympstone *(see page 116)*. Since 1985 the Commandant General has been an honorary member of the Company during his appointment.

Associations with Other Marine Corps

The Royal Marines have particularly close associations with the following Marine Corps of other countries:

The Royal Netherlands Marine Corps

Formed in 1665, during the Anglo-Dutch Wars, the Dutch Marines distinguished themselves both at sea and in raids on the English coast, where it is likely that they met their British counterparts. During the War of the Spanish Succession, when the two countries were allies, it was a combined force of British and Dutch Marines, under Prince George of Hesse-Darmstadt, which captured Gibraltar in 1704.

Today the Royal Netherlands Marine Corps, the Korps Mariniers, is an amphibious force with similar functions to the Royal Marines. It provides an Amphibious Combat Group in the Netherlands Antilles, in addition to its major commitment with the United Kingdom/Netherlands Landing Force, with which it deploys a further Amphibious Combat Group, a Special Boats Section and a Landing Craft Detachment. This integration and cooperation, unique in NATO, was seen in 1991 during operations in Eastern Turkey and Northern Iraq.

The motto *QUA PATET ORBIS* (Wherever the World Extends) symbolises the service of the Corps throughout the world during its long history. A greetings message is sent to the RNLMC, the senior corps in the Netherlands armed forces, on the occasion of its birthday each year, 10th December.

The United States Marine Corps

Detachments of Continental Marines served on board several warships that were fitted out on the orders of George Washington in the Autumn of 1775. These formed the basis of two battalions of Marines which were raised later that year to serve during the American War of Independence and were the forerunners of today's United States Marine Corps.

The United States Marine Corps and the Royal Marines have fought side by side on numerous occasions. In particular in China in 1900, during the Boxer Rebellion, both during the Siege of the Peking Legations and in the relief force. During the Korean War, 41 Independent Commando RM served under the command of the 1st US Marine Division and, for its part in the fighting at Chosin Reservoir in November 1950, the unit was awarded the US Presidential Citation. The association between the two Corps is today stronger than ever, with the cross posting of officers and NCOs and attendance on each other's training courses.

The Corps football trophy, the Tunney Cup, (named after world boxing champion Lt Col Gene Tunney) was presented by the USMC in 1929 and is competed for annually by the RM units. Their badge also includes the globe, but depicts the Western Hemisphere, and their motto is *SEMPER FIDELIS* (Always Faithful). A greetings message is sent to the USMC, the oldest military body in the United States, on the occasion of its birthday each year, 10th November.

Associations with Other Regiments

The Royal Marines have particular associations with the following Regiments:

The Princess of Wales's Royal Regiment
(Queen's and Royal Hampshire)

The Princess of Wales's Royal Regiment was formed by an amalgamation of a number of regiments which included the Queen's Royal Regiment (West Surrey) and the East Surrey Regiment. Although both Surrey regiments served as marines during their early history, the Royal Marines particular connection was with the East Surreys. This was founded on a disaster in 1825 which befell half the regiment whilst on passage to India. Fire broke out in their ship during a violent gale in the Bay of Biscay and after abandoning ship the survivors, including many women and children, were transported to Chatham where they were befriended by the Royal Marines. Today Officers and Warrant Officers Class 1 of the Princess of Wales's Royal Regiment wear a Blue Lanyard, a custom which originated in the East Surrey Regiment. A message of greetings is sent to the 1st Battalion each year on the anniversary of the Battle of the Glorious First of June in 1794, when the Queen's Royal Regiment (West Surrey) were embarked in ships of the Royal Navy.

The Argyll and Sutherland Highlanders

Early connections date from Balaclava in the Crimean War and Lucknow during the Indian Mutiny, but the main association stems from World War 2. In July 1940, after the fall of Dunkirk, the 8th Battalion, Argyll and Sutherland Highlanders served with the Royal Marine Brigade for over a year. When HMS *Prince of Wales* and *Repulse* were sunk in December 1941, the Royal Marines survivors joined up with the remnants of the 2nd Battalion, in the defence of Singapore. They formed what became known as 'The Plymouth Argylls', after the association football team, since both ships were Plymouth manned. Most of the Highlanders and Marines who survived the bitter fighting were taken prisoner by the Japanese. The Royal Marines inter-unit rugby football trophy is the 'Argyll Bowl', presented to the Corps by the Regiment in 1947. A message of greetings is sent to the Regiment each year on their Regimental Day, 25th October, the anniversary of the Battle of Balaclava in 1854.

Australian Army
The Royal New South Wales Regiment and the 1st Commando Regiment

Elements of the predecessors of the Royal New South Wales Regiment served alongside the Royal Marine Battalion in the Sudan Campaign in 1885. Members of the Regiment were at Gallipoli and in France. In World War II a great many officers and men served with distinction side by side with Royal Marines units in Crete in 1941.

Independent Companies were raised in Australia in 1941 and carried out commando training. Although these units were disbanded after the war, two commando companies were later reformed and one of these was enlarged and re-designated the 1st Infantry Battalion (Commando) (The City of Sydney's Own Regiment). The Royal Marines were closely connected with the training of officers and NCOs for these units and in 1960 HM The Queen approved alliances between the Corps and the 1st Infantry Battalion (Commando) and between 45 Commando RM and the 2nd Commando Company. A new alliance was approved later with the Royal New South Wales Regiment, and this has been extended to 1 Commando Regiment also. Annual greetings messages are sent on 6th March, the anniversary of the commencement of commando training in Australia in 1941.

Barbados Defence Force

Close links have existed between the Royal Marines and the Barbados Defence Force since 1985 when a bond was established following a series of cross-training exercises in the Caribbean. The alliance was approved by HM The Queen in 1992 and confirmed at a ceremony on 14th August 1993 in Bridgetown, Barbados, attended by the Commandant General. Annual greetings are exchanged on the anniversary of the parade.

141

Regimental Music

Quick March: "A Life on the Ocean Wave" was composed by Henry Russell in 1868, with words by an American, Epps Sargent. A part of the song "The Sea" is included as the trio. Officially authorised as the Regimental Quick March in 1882, the original arrangement was by J A Kappey, then the Bandmaster of the Chatham Division. The version in use today dates from 1944 and is by Major F J Ricketts, the Director of Music of the Plymouth Division, better known as the march composer, Kenneth Alford.

A life on the ocean wave,
A home on the rolling deep,
Where the scatter'd waters rave
And the winds their revels keep.
Like an eagle caged, I pine
On this dull unchanging shore;
Oh give me the flashing brine,
The spray and the tempest's roar.

The Captain General receives the score of The Preobrajensky March
from Earl Mountbatten in Tercentenary Year, 1964

Slow March: The score of "The Preobrajensky March" was presented to the Corps in Tercentenary Year 1964 by Earl Mountbatten of Burma whose uncle, the Grand Duke Sergius, at one time commanded the Russian Preobrajensky Guards. Lord Mountbatten was a Colonel Commandant of the Royal Marines from 1965 until his assassination in 1979. The official arrangement of the march was made by Lieutenant Colonel F Vivian Dunn.
Salute: The first eight bars of "The Preobrajensky March" are played in quick time as a salute for Royal Marines General Officers.

Commando March: In addition to the Regimental Quick March, Commando units may use "Sarie Marais", an old South African trekking song much used by the Boer Commandos. During World War II it was often sung on the march by the Commandos and was particularly popular with the officers of the Union of South Africa Defence Force seconded to the Royal Marines. Captain Vivian Dunn had made an arrangement of it for military band in 1937, but it was not officially adopted by the Corps until 1952. The Afrikaans translation is:

> *O take me back to the Old Transvaal*
> *That's where I long to be,*
> *I left my little Sarie where the mealies grow*
> *Just by the green thorn tree.*
> *And there I'll be to meet her where*
> *I loved her so.*
> *Down by the green thorn tree.*

Inspection Music: "The Globe and Laurel". This march was the regimental slow march until 1964. It is an arrangement by Vivian Dunn of the traditional old English air, "Early One Morning" which he composed in 1935, for ceremonial use when the Royal Marines first carried out Public Duties in London.

Much of the Regimental Music of the Royal Marines has been composed or arranged by Vivian Dunn who, in 1931, had the unique distinction of being appointed Director of Music of Portsmouth Division, direct from civilian life, the last military musician to do so. In 1953 he became the first Principal Director of Music of the Royal Marines and retired in 1968 as Lieutenant Colonel Sir Vivian Dunn KCVO OBE FRAM RM having been the only Director of Music in any Service to be knighted. He died in 1995.

143

Appendix O

Nicknames & Sayings

Jollies – This was the nickname of the Trained Bands of the City of London, who provided many of the recruits for the first regiment formed for service at sea. It is a term seldom used today but is to be found in Rudyard Kipling's famous poem "Soldier an' Sailor too" *(see page 159)* and Kenneth Alford's well known march composition "H.M. Jollies". At one time a Royal Marine was often called 'Joey', although the term eventually died out, the subaltern of a ship's RM detachment was usually referred to as 'Young Joe', whilst the officer commanding the detachment was always 'Major', and the senior NCO was known as 'Sergeant Major', regardless of his rank.

Royal – Naval mess-deck slang for a Royal Marine. Naval officers normally referred to their RM counterparts as 'Soldier'.

Lobsters – A very old nickname for a soldier because of their scarlet tunics. The RMLI, known as 'The Red Marines', were therefore 'Lobsters', whilst the RMA, 'The Blue Marines' were 'Unboiled Lobsters', all terms seldom heard today. Bluejackets also used to call Marines 'Turkeys'.

Les Petits Grenadiers – In the 18th and 19th century Grenadiers were amongst the tallest and bravest men in a battalion. At the capture of Belle Isle in 1761, the headdress of the Marines was very similar but smaller than that worn by Grenadiers. Although of normal stature, their fighting ability and behaviour in battle were exemplary, resulting in the French referring to them as 'Les petits Grenadiers'.

Bootneck – A term deriving its origins from the leather 'stock' worn round the neck inside the collar by soldiers. Sailors goaded Marines by saying *"Take my sea boots off your neck"*, implying that a piece had been cut from his boots to serve as a stock.. The expression is now used widely to mean a Royal Marine.

Leatherneck – A term having the same origin as 'Bootneck' but normally applied to the United States Marine and it is the title of their monthly magazine.

Dead Marine – Means an empty wine bottle. Lt Col W P Drury RMLI, a noted writer of naval stories and playwright, relates that the Duke of

Clarence used the expression at a dinner party and when a Colonel of Marines looked annoyed, the future King William IV explained that 'He has done his duty once, and is ready to do it again'.

Tell It To The Marines – Often used with a sneer, as though it meant that only a Marine would be credulous enough to believe it. Colonel Drury wrote on the contrary that it was a test of truth as Marines, who served all over the world could verify or belie any 'wild' story. Sir Walter Scott used the expression in 'Red Gauntlet' (1824) and Lord Byron in 'The Island' (1823).

Horse Marines – An expression giving an idea of incongruity, from the absurd thought of mounted men on board ship. Nevertheless over the years Marines have often carried out mounted duties ashore. However the term is likely to have originated from two troops of the 17th Light Dragoons (now the Queen's Royal Lancers) which served afloat in HMS *Success* in the West Indies in 1795, but whether in fact they acted as Marines is not known.

Appendix P

The Royal Marines Museum

The Museum of the Corps is housed in the former Officers' Mess of Eastney Barracks at Southsea, Hampshire, originally the home of the Royal Marine Artillery and later of Portsmouth Division Royal Marines. Open all the year round and seven days a week, within the stately building, displays tell the story of the Royal Marines from 1664 to the present day. There are rooms devoted to both early and contemporary history, arctic warfare and the Royal Marines Band Service. The Medal Room houses over 5,000 medals, including all the ten Victoria Crosses won by members of the Corps. There are many tableaux, audio visual displays and cases devoted to badges, sporting achievements, humour and other Marine Corps. Also on display is a large collection of paintings and silverware.

On the extensive lawns outside there is a junior commando assault course, landing craft and historical weapons. Inside is a comprehensive gift shop and light refreshments are available in *The Bugle Major* restaurant. An extensive archive department is available to researchers by prior appointment and this includes a historical library and a large photographic collection.

Appendix Q

Mess Customs

The King's Candlesticks

On 21st December 1949, not long after his title changed from Colonel-in-Chief to Captain General Royal Marines, HM King George VI presided at a dinner of the Officers of the Corps at the Savoy Hotel, London. For the occasion each Royal Marines Officers' Mess provided a pair of candelabra. The candles were lit just before the Loyal Toast. His Majesty expressed a wish that, in future at formal dinners, after the table had been cleared and the port passed, other lighting should be dimmed and the King's Candles lit in what is an exclusive ceremony to the Royal Marines.

The Loyal Toast

On 23rd July 1964, to mark the Tercentenary of the formation of the Admiral's Regiment, HM Queen Elizabeth II dined with the Officers of the Royal Marines. The dinner, at which HRH The Duke of Edinburgh, as Captain General, presided, was held at the Royal Naval College, Greenwich. It was on this occasion that, at the instigation of Admiral of the Fleet, the Earl Mountbatten of Burma (then Chief of the Defence Staff and the following year to be appointed a Colonel Commandant Royal Marines), Her Majesty granted the Royal Marines the privilege of drinking the Loyal Toast seated, when in their own messes. This privilege extends also to the Sergeants' Messes and those of Junior Non-Commissioned Officers.

Toast to the Captain General

Immediately following the Loyal Toast, the President proposes the toast to the Captain General. This toast is also drunk seated.

When his Majesty King George VI was on the throne the Loyal Toast was proposed as "The King, Our Captain General".

Specialist Qualification Badges

Pilot
(Navy Trained)

Pilot
(Army Trained)

Aircrewman

Parachutist

Sniper

Bugler

Musician

Tradesman

Telecommunications
Technician

Medical
Assistant

Classes in all the qualifications below are denoted by:
1st Class – a crown above the badge
2nd Class – a star above and a star below the badge
3rd Class – a star above the badge

Drill/Platoon
Weapons

Drivers

Letters in the wreath denote:
HW – Heavy Weapons
AE – Assault Engineer
LC – Landing Craft
MP – Military Police
SC – Swimmer Canoeist
ML – Mountain Leader
SA – Stores Accountant
K – Chef
C – Clerk

Physical
Training

Signallers

Lanyards

Coloured lanyards are worn on the right shoulder by all ranks serving in the units listed below. These lanyards are not worn in blue uniform.

Maroon.....................................Headquarters UK Amphibious Force
and the staff of the Director Royal Marines
Green...............................Headquarters 3 Commando Brigade and the UK
Landing Force Command Support Group
Light Blue...40 Commando RM
White...42 Commando RM
Red..45 Commando RM
Navy Blue..Commando Logistic Regiment RM
Old Gold and Rifle Green ....539 Assault Squadron RM
Old Gold and Scarlet...Fleet Protection Group RM

All Officers and WO1s wear a navy blue silk lanyard on the left shoulder in most orders of dress.
Recruits in the King's Squad *(see page 134)* by custom wear a white double cord white lanyard on the left shoulder in blue uniform.

Appendix T

The Green Beret

During the early days of Commandos, ranks continued to wear their own regimental headdress and cap badge. There were 79 different badges being worn in No 1 Commando alone! In 1942, the officers of this Commando decided that matters should be regularised and that a beret would be most practicable. The Royal Tank Regiment had worn a black beret for many years and the recently formed Parachute Regiment had chosen a maroon beret. No 1 Commando wore a flash on their arm depicting a green salamander going through fire, which gave a choice between green, red and yellow. Green was deemed to be the most suitable. Their submission to the Chief of Combined Operations was forwarded by Lord Mountbatten to the Under-Secretary of State for War in a letter of 1st May 1942 and the first issue to Royal Marines Commandos was made in October that year. A local firm of tam-o-shanter makers in Irvine (Ayrshire) produced a beret made from some green cloth of the colour still worn today.

Royal Marines Association

"Once a Marine always a Marine"

Patron: Her Majesty The Queen

The Royal Marines Association which was formed in 1946, seeks to bring benefit to its members and to play a vibrant and supportive part in the life of the Corps Family. Its objectives are to maintain and promote esprit de corps and comradeship amongst all Royal Marines, past and present; to help and keep them in touch with one another and with the activities of the Corps by the formation of Branches at home and overseas; also to support Service charities which benefit Royal Marines, their families and dependants. Additionally, the Association works in partnership with Countermarch, the Royal Marines resettlement network, to provide a focal point for resettlement advice and job vacancies.

The strength of the Association is some 10,000 with about 78 branches in the UK and 11 overseas, divided between Australia, New Zealand and Canada, plus a contact in South Africa. The links with the serving Corps are particularly strong. The President is normally appointed one of the Colonels Commandant, whilst the Chairman is a Trustee of the Royal Marines Benevolent Fund and the Chief Executive is a member of the Globe and Laurel Management Committee. About 4,500 of the serving Corps are members of the Association.

The Association therefore provides the backbone of the 'cradle to grave' membership of the Corps Family and through it its members enjoy a number of special privileges and benefits. There is a continuous programme of social functions, visits and other events, as well as annual reunions, such as the two-days at CTCRM. There are also regular ceremonial remembrance parades, in London, elsewhere in the UK and, occasionally, abroad.

RMA Central Office, Eastney Esplanade, Southsea, Hants PO4 9PX
Telephone: 023 9273 1978   **Freephone:** 0800 169 6347
Fax: 023 9229 6945   **e-mail:** gensec@rma.org.uk

The Royal Marines Reserve

Formed in 1948 as the Royal Marine Forces Volunteer Reserve, the Royal Marines Reserve is a force of volunteers, similar to the Territorial Army, who carry out commando training in their spare time. Their role is to provide trained reinforcements to bring regular Royal Marines units up to full war establishment on mobilisation or operational deployment. The Reserve also provides certain specialist sections. The total strength is nearly a thousand all ranks.

Reservists train for a total of 36 days per year in their spare time, during evenings and at weekends. They also carry out 14 days continuous training annually. Initial training usually takes about one year, which includes two periods of two weeks at the Commando Training Centre Royal Marines at Lympstone and on completion of this they can then specialise in many of the skills open to regular Royal Marines. Units and detachments are located throughout the country:

RMR City of London	is at Bermondsey and has detachments at Chatham, Portsmouth and Henley-on-Thames
RMR Scotland	is in Glasgow and has detachments at Dundee and Greenock.
RMR Bristol	has detachments at Cardiff, Plymouth, Poole and Lympstone.
RMR Merseyside	is at Birkenhead and has detachments at Birmingham and Rochdale.
RMR Tyne	is in Newcastle upon Tyne, but has no detachments.

Appendix W

Cadets

Marine Detachments of the Sea Cadet Corps

The present Sea Cadet Corps was established in 1899, but was not recognised by the Admiralty until 20 years later when the present title was adopted. In 1955, at the instigation of the Commandant General Royal Marines, a number of Marine Cadet Sections were formed to fit into the existing organisation of the thriving Sea Cadet Corps. Today there are almost a hundred Marine Detachments.

Besides carrying out both military and nautical training, which reflects the Royal Marines connection, marine cadets learn to operate as a team, develop leadership skills and how to become a responsible citizen in today's society. Most units operate the Duke of Edinburgh's Award scheme and adventurous training is a major item in Sea Cadet Corps programmes.

Royal Marines Detachments of the Combined Cadet Force

Cadet units were established to support the Volunteer force formed in the army in the late 1850s and provide a source of recruits for them. In 1908 the cadets were reorganised into two divisions of the Officers' Training Corps. In 1940 the junior division was retitled the Junior Training Corps and in 1945, when the JTC was reorganised as the Combined Cadet Force, Naval and Air Sections were incorporated. In September 1980 Royal Marines Detachments were formed within ten of the Naval sections and this has been expanded to almost twenty schools.

The Royal Marines Detachments are broadly organised on a troop structure, with three sections of eight. The cadets learn all basic military skills such as drill, fieldcraft, administration and minor tactics. They can also cover subjects such as unarmed combat, survival skills, mountain and arctic warfare, more complex tactics, scuba diving and parachuting. The detachments offer the cadets an opportunity to develop useful skills such as teamwork, leadership and the ability to work in groups whilst also gaining an insight into the Royal Marines.

Royal Marines Volunteer Cadet Corps

The first Cadet Corps in the Royal Marines was formed at Eastney in 1901 and two years later units were established at Chatham, Gosport, Plymouth and Deal, whilst similar naval cadet units also existed at their Port Divisions. Originally RM cadets were all sons of members of the Corps but in 1922 recruiting was opened to other boys. Disbanded during the Second World War they were re-formed again in 1945.

There are at present units at Portsmouth, Plymouth and Lympstone and each one is autonomous. Commanded by a Royal Marines officer appointed by the Commanding Officer of the parent regular unit, they have serving other ranks and civilians as instructors.

Cadets are aged between 9 and 18, dependent on the rules in each unit and priority of entry is given to children of serving and former members of the RN and RM, but others may be considered if vacancies exist. Girls Ambulance Companies had existed before the Second World War, but today in some of the RMVCC units entry is open to girls.

151

Appendix X

Bibliography

The following books provide recommended reading on the history of the Royal Marines. and the majority should be available through any public library. They can also be consulted by making an appointment to use the reading room in the library of the Royal Marines Museum at Eastney.

Beadle, Maj J C – *The Light Blue Lanyard. 50 Years with 40 Commando RM* (Published Privately 1992)

Beaver, Paul – *Today's Royal Marines* (Patrick Stevens 1988).

Blumberg, Gen. Sir H E – *Britain's Sea Soldiers, 1914-19* (Swift & Co. 1927)

Brooks, Richard – *The Royal Marines – 1664 to the Present* (Constable, 2002)

Bruce Lockhart, Sir Robert – *The Marines Were There* (Putnam, 1950)

Clapp, Michael / Southby-Tailyour Ewen – *Amphibious Assault Falklands.- The Battle of San Carlos Water.* (Orion 1996)

Crockett, Maj Anthony – *Green Beret, Red Star* (Eyre & Spottiswood, 1954)

Edye, Major L – *Historical Records Of The Royal Marines Vol 1* (Harrison, 1893)

Field, Colonel Cyril – *Britain's Sea Soldiers* (Lyceum Press, 1924)

Ford, Ken – D-Day Commando. *From Normandy to the Maas with 48 RM Commando* (Sutton Publishing, 2003)

Forfar, John – *From Omaha to the Sheldt. The Story of 47 RM Commando* (Tuckwell Press, 2001)

Foster, Nigel – *Making of a Royal Marine Commando* (Sidgwick & Jackson, 1987)

Fraser E and Carr-Laughton L G – *The Royal Marine Artillery* (RUSI, 1930)

Grover, Colonel G – *Short History of the Royal Marines* (Gale & Polden,. 2nd Edition 1959)

Hampshire, A Cecil – *The Royal Marines Tercentenary* (The Commandant General Royal Marines 1964)

Hayhurst, Fred – *Green Berets In Korea* (Vanguard Press, 2003.)

HMSO – *The Royal Marines. The Admiralty record of their achievements 1939-1943.*

Jenkins, W G – *Commando Subaltern at War. RM Operations in Yugoslavia and Italy 1944/45.* (Greenhill 1996)

Ladd, James D – *By Sea By Land. The Authorised History of the Royal Marines Commandos* (Harper Collins 1999)

Ladd, James D – *Royal Marine Commando* (Hamlyn, 1982)

Ladd, James – *Commandos and Rangers of World War II* (Macdonald and Jane's, 1978)

Ladd, James D – *Inside the Commandos* (Arms and Armour Press, 1984)

Lane, Andrew – *The Royal Marines Barracks Eastney – A Pictorial History.* (Halsgrove 1998)

Lane, Andrew – *Royal Marines Deal – A Pictorial History* (Halsgrove 2000)

Lane, Andrew – *Royal Marines Commandos in the Falklands War – A Pictorial History* (Halsgrove 2000)

Little, Matthew Grant – *The Royal Marines & The Victoria Cross* (RM Museum 2002)

Marsh, Major A E – Flying Marines (Privately published 1980)

McConville, Michael – *Nothing Much To Lose. The Story of 2nd Battalion Royal Marines and 43 Commando Royal Marines* (Published privately 1992).

Mackenzie, Tony – *44(RM) Commando – Achnacarry to the Arakan. A Diary of the Commando at War, August 1943 to March 1947* (Tom Donovan, 1996)

Mitchell, Raymond – *They Did What Was Asked Of Them – 41 (Royal Marines) Commando 1942-1946* (Firebird Books, , 1996.)

Moulton, J L – *The Royal Marines* (RM Museum, 1981)

Moulton, J L – *Haste to the Battle: A Marine Commando at War.* (Cassell, 1963)

Neillands, Robin – *By Sea and Land* (Weidenfeld & Nicholson, 1987)

Nicolas, Paul H – *Historical Record of the Royal Marine Forces* (Boone, 1845)

Nutting, David (Editor) – *Attain by Surprise – The Story of 30 Assault Unit – Royal Navy/Royal Marine Commando – Intelligence by Capture in WW II* (David Colver, 1997)

Oakley, Derek and Smith, Peter C – *The Royal Marines* (Spellmount, 1988)

Oakley, Captain Derek – *The Royal Marines into the Nineties* (Commandant General Royal Marines 1993)

Oakley, Derek – *Fiddler On The March – A Biography of Lt Col Sir Vivian Dunn* (RM Historical Society, 2000).

Oakley, Derek – *The Commandos. World War Two to the Present* (Arms and Armour Press, 1987)

Phillips, C E Lucas – *Cockleshell Heroes* (Heineman, 1956).

Reynolds, David – *Commando – The Illustrated History of Britain's Green Berets from Dieppe to Afghanistan* (Sutton, 2001)

Rose, Colonel Markham – *The Story of the Royal Marines* (Seventh edition 1935)

Smith, Peter C – *Per Mare Per Terram* (Balfour, 1974)

Southby-Tailyour, Ewen – *Reasons in Writing. A Commando's View of the Falklands War* (Leo Cooper, 1993)

Stadden, Newark and Donald – *Uniforms of The Royal Marines from 1664 to the Present Day* (Pompadour Gallery, 1997)

Thomas, Gareth – *Records Of The Royal Marines. PRO Readers' Guide No. 10* (PRO Publications, 1994)

Thompson, Julian – *The Royal Marines. From Sea Soldiers to a Special Force* (Sidgwick & Jackson, 2000).

Thompson, Julian – *No Picnic. 3 Commando Brigade in the South Atlantic: 1982* (Leo Cooper/Secker and Warburg, 1985)

Trendell, John – *Colonel Bogey to the Fore* (The Blue Band Magazine, 1991).

Vaux, Nick – *March to the South Atlantic* (Buchan and Enright 1986)

Young, David – *Four Five. The Story of 45 Commando RM 1943-1971* (Leo Cooper, 1972)

Young, John Robert – *The Royal Marines* (Bantam, 1991)

The Royal Marines (Pitkin Pictorials Ltd, 1971)

The Royal Marines Museum. The Story of Britain's Sea Soldiers (RM Museum, 1989)

1664-1964. An Account of the Royal Marines Tercentenary Celebrations (Privately published 1964)

A History of the Royal Marines Reserve 1948-1979 (Privately published 1979)

A Brief Chronology of Principal Events

1664 – Formation of the Duke of York and Albany's Maritime Regiment of Foot.

1665-72 – 2nd & 3rd Dutch Wars. Royal Netherlands Marine Corps formed.

1685 – Renamed Prince George of Denmark's Regiment – disbanded 1689

1689-97 – War with France

1702-13 – War of Spanish Succession. Six Regts of Marines formed

1704 – British and Dutch Marines capture Gibraltar.

1713 – Reduced to three Regiments which were transferred to the Line. Only four Companies of Marine Invalids remained

1739 – England declared war on Spain – The War of Jenkins' Ear. Six Marine Regiments raised

1740 – Further four Regiments raised

1745-1750 – Hannah Snell, served in the Marines.

1748 – The Peace of Aix-la-Chapelle. All ten Marine Regiments disbanded

1755 – A permanent Marine Corps of 50 Independent Companies established. Corps Strength 5,000

1756 – The Seven Years War. Corps Strength 19,000

1759 – The Capture of Quebec.

1761 – The Capture of Belle Isle.

1770 – Marines land with Captain James Cook at Botany Bay, Australia.

1775 – American War of Independence. The Battle of Bunker Hill. United States Marine Corps formed.

1776 – Corps Strength 25,000

1783 – Stonehouse Barracks first occupied.

1788 – Marines from the First Fleet land in Australia.

1793-1802 – French Revolutionary Wars – Actions in the Mediterranean, South Africa, India, Egypt and the East Indies.

1794 – The Battle of the Glorious First of June off Ushant.

1797 – The Battles of Camperdown and Cape St Vincent.

1798 – The Battle of the Nile.

1802 – The Corps honoured with the title 'Royal'.

1803-15 – Napoleonic Wars – Actions in East and West Indies, South America, South Africa and others.

1804 – RM Artillery Companies formed.

1805 – The Battle of Trafalgar. Woolwich Division formed. Corps Strength 31,000

1812-15 – The War of 1812 in America

1814 – The sacking of Washington

1815 – Napoleon exiled to St Helena

1816 – The bombardment of Algiers

1820 – King George IV directed RM would take precedence after 49th Regt.

1827 – Colours presented to each of the Divisions by HRH The Duke of Clarence. 'The Globe' badge granted. Corps Strength 9,000

1835-40 – RM Battalion and RMA Battery in Spain during the Carlist War.

1839-42 – RM in action in China's Opium wars.

1848 – Portsmouth Division moved into Forton Barracks, Gosport.

1854-56 – The Crimean War

1854 – Battle of Inkerman – first Royal Marine awarded VC – Cpl Prettyjohns.

1855 – Royal Marines designated Light Infantry. Corps Strength 15,500.

1856-60 – 2nd China War

1857-58 – Indian Mutiny

1861 – Depot established at Deal.

1861-64 – The Maori Wars in New Zealand

1861-62 – RM Battalion in Mexico

1862 – RMA & RMLI became separate Corps

1864 – Eastney Barracks first occupied

1864-65 – RM Battalion in Japan

1867-68 – Expedition to Abyssinia

1868 – RM Battalion in Ireland

1869 – Woolwich Division closed.

1870 – RM Battalion in Japan

1873-74 – The Ashanti War

1879 – The Zulu War

1880-83 – RM Battalion in Ireland

1882 – The Egyptian Campaign

1884-85 – The Sudan Campaign

1899-1902 – RM with the Naval Brigade in South Africa. Corps Strength 19,000

1900-01 – RM in action during the Boxer Rebellion alongside the USMC (for the first time).

1903 – Royal Naval School of Music formed at Eastney. RM Memorial in the Mall unveiled

1914-18 - First World War. Marines in HM Ships in all major engagements at sea.

1914 – RM Brigade at Ostend and Antwerp.

1915 – RM Brigade with the RN Division in Gallipoli. RMA Howitzer and AA. Bdes & Heavy Siege Train to France and Flanders.

1916 – RM Battalions to France with 63rd (RN) Division. Battle of Jutland.

1918 – The Raid on Zeebrugge – 4th RM Battalion. Institution of King's Squad & King's Badge. Corps Strength 55,000

1919 – 6th Battalion in North Russia.

1922 – 8th Battalion in Ireland

1923 – 11th Battalion in Turkey. Amalgamation of RMA and RMLI. Forton Barracks, Gosport closed.

1927 – 12th Battalion in Shanghai.

1930 – RN School of Music moved to Deal.

1935 – RM carryout London Duties London for the first time. RM in Alexandria with Base Defences, Mediterranean. Corps Strength 9,800

1939-45 – Second World War. Marines in HM Ships in all major engagements at sea.

1940 – RM ashore in Faroe Islands, Iceland, Norway, Holland and France.

1941 – MNBDO1 in the evacuation of Crete. HMS *Prince of Wales* and *Repulse* sunk.

1942 – 'Plymouth Argylls' in Singapore. Force VIPER in Burma.

First RM Commando formed.

40 RM Commando at Dieppe.

11th RM Battalion at Tobruk.

Op Frankton – Cockleshell Heroes raid on Bordeaux shipping.

1943 – 40 & 41 Commandos land in Sicily. 41 Commando landed at Salerno. RM Battalions formed into Commandos. 40 & 43 Commandos in action in Italy, Albania and Yugoslavia.

1944 – 43 Commando landed at Anzio. 48 Commando formed. 17,500 Marines in The Landings in Normandy serving in Commandos, HM Ships and Landing Craft. 41,47 & 48 Cdos in the Assault on Walcheren, supported by Marines in HM Ships and landing craft.

1945 – 42 & 44 Commandos in the Battle of Kangaw, Burma. 40 & 43 Commandos in the Battle of Lake Comacchio, Italy. RM Commandos in the river crossings in NW Europe. Corps Strength 78,500

1946 – Marines from HM Ships occupy Penang. 42 & 44 Commandos occupy Hong Kong.

1947 – Reorganisation of the Corps – RM Divisions become functional Groups.

1948 – RM Commandos cover the withdrawal from Palestine and deployed in the Suez Canal Zone. RM Forces Volunteer Reserve formed.

1949 – 45 Commando in Egyt and Aqaba. 3 Commando Brigade moves to Hong Kong. Closure of Chatham Group.

1950 – 3 Commando Brigade moved to Malaya. 41 Independent Commando formed for operations in Korea. Chatham Barracks closed. RM Divisional Bands integrated with the RN School of Music to form the Royal Marines School of Music.

1952 – 3 Commando Brigade moved to Malta. Presentation of first Colours to the RM Commandos. 41 Independent Commando disbanded at Bickleigh.

1953 – 3 Commando Brigade moved to the Suez Canal Zone. HRH The Duke of Edinburgh appointed Captain General Royal Marines.

1954 – 40 & 45 Commandos returned to Malta. 42 Commando moves to UK Amphibious School RM moved to Poole

1955-59 – 40 & 45 Commandos alternated on operations in Cyprus.

1956 – 3 Commando Brigade spearheaded landings at Port Said. First RM detachments for frigates formed. Corps Strength 10,000

1957 – Elements of 42 Commando in Northern Ireland. Small Arms School RM at Browndown closed.

1958 – RM Gunnery School at Eastney closed.

1960 – HMS *Bulwark* commissioned as first Commando Ship. 45 Commando moved to Aden. 42 Commando moved to Singapore. 41 Commando re-formed. Melville Barracks Chatham closed. Green Berets to be worn by all trained ranks.

1961 – 42 & 45 Commandos landed in Kuwait. HQ 3 Commando Brigade established in Singapore. 43 Commando re-formed in Plymouth.

1962 – 40 & 42 Commandos in Brunei. Limbang Operation.

1963-66 – 3 Commando Brigade (less 45 Commando) in anti-terrorist Confrontation operations in Borneo and Malaysia.

156

1964 – 41 & 45 Commandos in East Africa. Corps Tercentenary celebrations. Lovat Dress introduced.

1964-1967 – 45 Commando on operations in the Radfan.

1965 – Earl Mountbatten of Burma appointed a Colonel Commandant RM

1966 – The RMFVR retitled Royal Marines Reserve. End of Indonesian Confrontation.

1967 – 42 Commando covered the final withdrawal from Aden. 45 Commando returned to UK. 40 Commando on IS duties in Hong Kong

1968 – 43 Commando disbanded.

1969 – 41 Commando was the first RM Commando on operations in Northern Ireland

1970 – 45 Commando assigned to NATO for the Northern Flank.

1971 – 3 Commando Brigade returned to UK from the Far East. 41 Commando moved to Malta. 45 Commando moved to Arbroath.

1972 – Commando Logistic Regiment formed. Warrant rank reintroduced.

1973 – PRORM integrated with HMS Centurion.

1974 – 40 & 41 Commandos with UN Forces in Cyprus. Corps Strength 7,000

1976 – RM detachments in frigates during the Cod War off Iceland.

1977 – Silver Jubilee Inspection by HM The Queen on Plymouth Hoe. 41 Commando (less Salerno Company) left Malta.

1978 – First 10-man Frigate detachment formed. 41 Commando carried out London Duties.

1979 – Salerno Company left Malta.. 42 Commando deployed to Hong Kong for IS duties. Earl Mountbatten assassinated by the IRA.

1980 – Comacchio Company formed (later RM Fleet Protection Group) Elements of 42 Commando deployed to the New Hebrides (Vanuatu). 3rd Raiding Squadron deployed to Hong Kong for duties against illegal immigrants.

1981 – HRH Crown Prince Harald (now HM The King of Norway) appointed Honorary Colonel Royal Marines. 41 Commando disbanded at Deal. The Commandant General, Lt Gen Sir Steuart Pringle blown up outside his house by a terrorist car bomb.

1982 – 3 Commando Brigade spearheaded the recapture of the Falkland Islands. RM Detachment for NP 1002 first deployed to Diego Garcia. 3 Commando Brigade Air Squadron moved to RNAS Yeovilton.

1983 – 40 Commando deployed to Cyprus for UN tour of duty. RM Band of Flag Officer Naval Air Command disbanded. 40 Commando moved to Taunton.

1984 – Detachments of 3 Commando Brigade Air Defence Troop embarked in ships of the Armilla Patrol. HM The Queen visited RM Poole. 539 Assault Squadron formed. All 10-man Frigate detachments withdrawn.

1985-93 – RM Commandos deployed on operational tours in Belize.

1986 – 42 Commando carried out London Duties. RM Commando memorial unveiled at Lympstone.

1987 – RM Band of Flag Officer 3rd Flotilla (FOF3) disbanded.

SBS titled Special Boat Service and came under command of Director Special Forces.

1988 – 3rd Raiding Squadron disbanded in Hong Kong.

1989 – IRA bomb exploded at RMSM Deal killing 11 band ranks.

1990 – RM embarked in HM Ships during the Gulf War.

1991 – HQ Commando Forces and 3 Commando Brigade (less 42 Commando) deployed to South East Turkey for Operation Haven. Eastney Barracks closed.

1992 – Alliance with the Barbados Defence Force.

1994 – 45 Commando deployed to Kuwait.

1995 – Headquarters Royal Marines established on Whale Island, Portsmouth.

3 Commando Brigade Air Squadron incorporated into Naval Air Command as 847 Naval Air Sqn. RM provided the Commander and the Operations Staff of the Rapid Reaction Force HQ in Bosnia. Commando Logistic Regiment moved to Chivenor. 42 Commando and elements of the Commando Logistic Regiment on humanitarian and disaster relief in the West Indies. DRORM closed.

1996 – Royal Marines School of Music moved to Portsmouth.

1996-97 – 42 Commando and a detachment from 539 Squadron in the Congo prepared to evacuate civilians from Kinshasa.

1998 – 45 Commando on humanitarian and disaster relief in Honduras and Nicaragua. 40 Commando and a detachment from 539 Squadron in the Congo prepared to evacuate British Nationals

1999 – Ranks of RM officers aligned to those of the Army.

2000 – 42 Commando deployed to Sierra Leone. HQ 3 Commando Brigade, 45 Commando, the Commando Logistic Regiment and the RM Band Plymouth deployed to Kosovo. RM National Memorial in London unveiled. Comacchio Group renamed Fleet Protection Group RM

2001 – Fleet Protection Group moved from Arbroath to Faslane. New Colours presented to 40, 42 and 45 Commandos at Plymouth. Elements of 40 Commando deployed in HMS *Ocean* for operations in Afghanistan. 3 Commando Brigade Signal Squadron RM renamed United Kingdom Landing Force Command Support Group. RM Poole renamed 1 Assault Group.

2002 – 45 Commando Group deployed on operations in Afghanistan. Headquarters United Kingdom Amphibious Force established with the Commandant General as the Commander (COMUKAMPHIBFOR). Firefighters' Industrial action, over 600 RM ranks involved. Corps Strength 6,100

2003 – The Iraq War. Op TELIC – 3 Commando Brigade operations on the Al Faw peninsula and the liberation of Basra.

2004 – 40 Commando on operational tour in Iraq

"Soldier an' Sailor Too" *by Rudyard Kipling*

As I was spittin' into the Ditch aboard o' the Crocodile,
I seed a man on a man-o'-war got up in the Reg'lars' style.
'E was scrapin' the paint from off of 'er plates, an' I sez to 'im, "Oo are you?"
Sez'e, "I'm a Jolly – 'Er Majesty's Jolly – soldier an' sailor too!"
Now 'is work begins by Gawd knows when, and 'is work is never through;
'E isn't one o' the reg'lar Line, nor 'e isn't one of the crew.
'E's a kind of a giddy harumfrodite – soldier an' sailor too!
An', after, I met 'im all over the world, a-doin' all kinds of things,
Like landin' 'isself with a Gatlin' gun to talk to them 'eathen kings;
'E sleeps in an 'ammick instead of a cot, an' 'e drills with the deck on a slew,
An' 'e sweats like a Jolly -'Er Majesty's Jolly – soldier an' sailor too!
For there isn't a job on the top o' the earth the beggar don't know, nor do -
You can leave 'im at night on a bald man's 'ead, to paddle 'is own canoe
'Es a sort of a bloomin' cosmoplolouse – soldier an' sailor too.
We've fought 'em in trooper, we've fought 'em in dock, and drunk with 'em in betweens,
When they called us the seasick scull'ry-maids, an' we called 'em the Ass-Marines;
But, when we was down for a double fatigue, from Woolwich to Bernardmyo,
We sent for the Jollies – 'Er Majesty's Jollies – soldier an' sailor too!
They think for 'emselves, an' they steal for 'emselves, an' they never ask what's to do,
But they're camped an' fed an' they're up an' fed before our bugle's blew.
Ho! they ain't no limpin' procrastitutes – soldier an' sailor too.

You may say we are fond of an 'arness-cut, or 'ootin' in barrick-yards,
Or startin' a Board School mutiny along o' the Onion guards;
But once in a while we can finish in style for the ends of the earth to view,
The same as the Jollies – 'Er Majesty's Jollies – soldier an' sailor too!
They come of our lot, they was brothers to us; they was beggars we'd met an' knew;
Yes, barrin' an inch in the chest an' the arm, they was doubles o' me an' you;
For they weren't no special chrysanthemums – soldier an' sailor too!
To take your chance in the thick of a rush, with firing all about,
Is nothing so bad when you've cover to 'and, an' leave an' likin' to shout:
But to stand an' be still to the Birken'ead drill is a damn' tough bullet to chew,
An' they done it, the Jollies-'Er Majesty's Jollies-soldier an' sailor too!
Their work was done when it 'adn't begun; they was younger nor me an' you;
Their choice it was plain between drownin' in 'eaps an' bein' mopped by the screw,
So they stood an' was still to the Birken'ead drill, soldier an' sailor too!
We're most of us liars, we're 'arf of us thieves, an' the rest are as rank as can be,
But once in a while we can finish in style (which I 'ope it won't 'appen to me).
But it makes you think better o' you an' your friends, an' the work you may 'ave to do,
When you think o' the sinkin' Victorier's Jollies-soldier an' sailor too!
Now there isn't no room for to say ye don't know – they 'ave proved it plain and true-
That, whether it's Widow, or whether it's ship, Victorier's work is to do,
An' they done it, the Jollies – 'Er Majesty's Jollies – soldier an' sailor too!

RM Historical Society Publications

SP1	1978	*Hail And Farewell* by Wilfred Davey MBE BEM
SP2	1979	*Extracts from Royal Marine Records Pt 1 – 1755 to 1792* by Gen Sir H E Blumberg KCB
SP3	1981	*The Royal Marines and the Dockyards 1755 – 1949* by Wilfred Davey MBE BEM
SP4	1982	*Extracts from Royal Marine Records Pt 2-1793 to 1836* by Gen Sir H E Blumberg KCB
SP5	1982	*Extracts From Royal Marine Records Pt 3 – 1837 to 1914* by Gen Sir H E Blumberg KCB
SP6	1984	*The Ghost of a General And The Royal Marine Officers Of 1914* by Lt Col Donald Bittner USMCR
SP7	1985	*One Time Marine (A Bootneck's Tale)* by Haydn Jenkins.
SP8	1985	*41 Independent Commando RM – Korea 1950-1952* by Lt Col Peter Thomas RM
SP9	1986	*Royal Marines in East Devon* (The Story of Lympstone and Dalditch Camps) by Anthony J Perrett.
SP10	1987	*Expedition To Siberia 1919* (The Great War – Eastern Front) by Capt T H Jameson DSO RMLI
SP11	1988	*Marines of The First Fleet* (Australian Bicentennial) from the Journals of Pte Easty, Sgt Scott and Lt Clark
SP12	1990	*Memoirs of Sergeant Harry Wright* (Zeebrugge Aftermath)
SP13	1991	*Fidelity Will Haunt Me Till I Die* by Peter Kingswell
SP14	1992	*Royal Marines in Wales* by Anthony J Perrett
SP15	1993	*Royal Marines Spies of World War One Era* by Lt Col D F Bittner USMCR and Capt J M Coleby RM
SP16	1994	*Royal Marines and D-Day* Compiled by Capt the Rev D A Farquharson-Roberts
SP17	1995	*Something About St Ives* (Reminiscences of the Commando Mountain Warfare Centre) by Derek Yardley Wright
SP18	1996	*Behind Japanese Lines* (The Untold Story of Royal Marine Detachment 385) by Capt Derek Oakley MBE RM
SP19	1997	*The Royal Marines And Hong Kong* (Over 150 Years from 1840 to 1997) by Dr S S Richardson AO CBE MA LLD.
SP20	1998	*Marines From The Medway* (The Story behind their Memorials in the Medway Towns) by Lt Col Brian Edwards RM
SP21	1999	*Mutiny In Murmansk, 'The Hidden Shame'* (Royal Marines in North Russia 1918/19) by Maj V M Bentinck RM
SP22	2000	*At The Turn Of The Centuries* (An Anniversary Portrait of the Marines in the Royal Navy of 1700, 1800, 1900 and after) by Lt Col Brian Edwards RM
SP23	2001	*The Story Of Colours In The Royal Marines* by Maj Alastair J Donald RM
SP24	2002	*Bagged In World War 2.* (Two Tales of RM Prisoners of War) The Jim Fallace Story by John Ambler and the Diary of Benjamin Knapton
SP25	2002	*A Short History Of The Royal Marines* 1664 – 2003 (First Edition)
SP26	2002	*Officers of the Royal Marines in the Age of Sail* by Dr Donald F Bittner
SP27	2003	*Cyprus Crisis – 1955-56* (The Story of 'B' Troop 45 Commando Royal Marines) by Charles Hart
SP28	2003	*The Royal Marines Band Service* by John Ambler
SP29	2004	*A Short History of the Royal Marines* 1664 – 2004 (Second Edition)

Copies of all these publications are available from the Souvenir Shop,
The Royal Marines Museum, Southsea, Hants. PO4 9PX
Telephone: 023 9281 9385 Ext 222